Let Go, Fly Free

Follow your dreams and live the life you truly deserve

About the Author

Suzi Mussell was born in Wallington, Surrey, England in 1965. She was educated for her entire school life by nuns at the Roman Catholic school of St. Philomena's. She was always a free-spirited young girl who loved to sing and act, but equally loved to spend time out of doors in the woods and fields around her family home.

She left school at the tender age of seventeen, with a few O'levels, an A level in Art and a secretarial diploma, eager to get out into the world. Her first job was in central London working in the accounts department of a firm of solicitors, travelling at a time when the risk of IRA bombs was high.

Her career path would lead her into the world of Information Technology and financial software, and indeed that is the sector she stayed in for her entire working life, up until she gave up working in March 2019.

Her real desire was to be an actress but she only ever pursued that dream at an amateur level. In 1990, at the age of twenty-five, she joined ATG, an amateur theatre group based in Warlingham, Surrey and performed in many productions from farces to panto and musicals. It was her escape from 'real life'. That same year she married her first husband who was twenty-one years her senior. The marriage unsurprisingly only lasted eighteen months.

After spending a few years living with various family members she eventually moved down to Sussex and started her own Information Technology company. This was when she discovered a passion for in-line skating and spent many hours a day on Brighton and Hove seafront, outside in nature where she felt her happiest.

In 1999 she met her second husband and a year later, at the age of thirty-five, was pregnant with her first child, Georgina. She married in 2002 and her son Zachary was born in 2005.

In 2017 she fulfilled one of her lifelong dreams, by going to a free school and orphanage in Haiti 'Hope House Haiti', and directed the biblical story 'Ruth', with fifty of the children in just ten days.

It was after this trip that her marriage of seventeen years was to end. She found in Haiti a happiness that money could not buy, despite the hardships that poverty causes there. This was the beginning of her spiritual awakening.

She moved into a new house in the heart of the Sussex countryside and had everything she needed for a good life. But something was still missing – true happiness. In the months that followed she listened to many spiritual teachings and immersed herself in self-help books on subjects like 'How to love yourself' and 'How to become the best version of yourself'. In September 2018 she went to an Osho Tantra retreat in India which would help cleanse herself of all the emotional and sexual blocks that had built up in her life.

Sixteen months after moving into her new home Suzi took the bold decision to quit her job, buy a campervan and rent her house to travel the world in search of an unconditioned, fulfilled and happy life – and to write this book.

Preface

I first started writing a book about my life experience at the tender age of eighteen. I had what I would call not your normal kind of upbringing and I was drawn by the desire to write. I believe now I probably just wanted to be heard. I only ever wrote a few chapters and still have the typewritten pages to this day and they may yet form the beginnings of a second book.

Throughout the years of my life the hankering of writing remained with me and when I decided to make this journey it seemed to me to be the perfect opportunity to make that desire a reality. After all, I would have all the time in the world to write and indeed as I have been on this journey many a person has commented that I should write a book.

My story is a sharing, of just how an ordinary, everyday kind of woman makes a life changing decision. As the title suggests it's about letting go of a life that did not fulfil me to be free to pursue the life that I was meant to live, a truly fulfilling and happy life.

When my journey began, I had no idea what would happen or indeed what the outcome would be. But I had the belief that I would be a changed person, for the better, at the end of it. Now I realise that our life journey is continuously unfolding, there is always more to discover about ourselves and the world. My hope is that by sharing my whole, unedited experience, it may inspire you to change the course of your life. If that happens, I will feel I have made some small difference in this world.

My journey has gone beyond any of my expectations. Not only has it changed my present, I am healing wounds from the past and forging a new future, not just for myself but for others who are inspired to believe in themselves and follow their true path. I hope that I am setting an example for my children, showing them that there is always a choice in life to live how you desire and follow your dreams, whatever they maybe, without fear of any judgement from others.

When you don't follow your dreams and sacrifice yourself for the good of others you are passing on your soul wounds to the next generation. I'm breaking that pattern and I hope that in time to come my children will be grateful and proud of me for showing them a different way. If we do not find our purpose, we will pass the loss of ourselves down to the generations that come after us.

It does seem from the comments that I get on my social media channels that I am indeed an inspiration to many and this fills my soul with love and happiness.

I believe that we all have a story to tell that would inspire or empower others to change the course of their life for the better. All it takes is a desire and a belief in yourself that you can achieve anything you truly desire.

Some of the content of this story is sexually explicit and I did wonder whether I should publish it. But, without it, my story is not complete and I would be hiding behind the fear of other's judgement. I do wonder why, as a general rule, we are so conditioned to not talk about the one thing that is the most natural act of love in the world. Why is sexual intimacy such a taboo subject?

I quote from the book 'The Awakened Woman' by Tererai Trent – "A woman with awakened sexuality has cultivated love and respect for her body and the bodies of all living beings. She celebrates the power of her femininity and her ability to forge sacred connections and generative creativity. She embraces joy and pleasure, expands rather than shrinks into her environment".

So, I share this intimacy with the knowledge that there are many of you who have either experienced the same and can relate to my experiences or would indeed like to free yourself of the chains of shame that hold you back from expressing your true self.

Let Go, Fly Free

Dream the impossible dream
Right the unrightable wrong
And I know if I'll only be true
To this glorious quest
That my heart will be peaceful and calm
When I'm laid to my rest

Lyrics by Joe Darion from 'The Impossible Dream' (The Quest)

Let Go, Fly Free

Henry David Thoreau

Our truest life is when we are in dreams awake

All good things are wild and free

Not until we are lost do we understand ourselves

Live your beliefs and you can turn the world around

That man is rich whose pleasures are the cheapest

There is no remedy for love but to love more

Go confidently in the direction of your dreams and live the life you have imagined.

There are moments when all anxiety and stated toil are becalmed in the infinite leisure and response of nature

Let Go, Fly Free

Rumi

Run from what's comfortable

Forget safety

Live where you fear to live

Destroy your reputation

Be notorious.

Copyright © 2021 Suzette Mussell

The right of Suzette Mussell to be identified as the author has been asserted.

All rights reserved. No part of this book may be reproduced in any form, or by any electronic or mechanical means, including information storage and retrieval systems without permission in writing from the author.

ISBN 978-1-5272-9271-0

Let go Fly free first published by mindfulvanlife 2021

It was written in Scandinavia, Europe & Bali

Cover image by Suzette Mussell

Digital illustration and typography by

www.marymccarthydesign.co.uk

www.mindfulvanlife.com

Contents

- Chapter 1 21
  - Goodbye Conditioned Life - April 2019 21
- Chapter 2 25
  - A Trip to Haiti - January 2017 25
- Chapter 3 33
  - Meeting Ray - December 2017 33
- Chapter 4 41
  - New Beginnings 41
- Chapter 5 45
  - The love story continues - Jan 2018...... 45
- Chapter 6 53
  - Mt. Etna Sicily - April 2018.................. 53
- Chapter 7 67
  - The Van 67
- Chapter 8 69
  - A Tinder Date - July 2018 69
- Chapter 9 77
  - Osho Nisarga Tantra Retreat India - September 2018..................................... 77
- Chapter 10 91
  - The Inevitable.. 91

Chapter 11 97
  A man for Christmas - December 2018 97

Chapter 12 105
  Revealing my Plans 105

Chapter 13 107
  Breakfast on the beach - my Inner Submissive 107

Chapter 14 117
  Waiting for Love - or Lust? 117

Chapter 15 121
  'Meet Lucy' 121

Chapter 16 125
  Van Life Begins - April 2019 125

Chapter 17 137
  A Birthday Alone - May 2019 137

Chapter 18 141
  Letting Go 141

Chapter 19 145
  Toy Boy in Edinburgh 145

Chapter 20 151
  A Reality Check - June 2019 151

Chapter 21 153

- Europe beckons 153
- Chapter 22 161
  - Love and trust in the flow of life 161
- Chapter 23 165
  - Rejection 165
- Chapter 24 169
  - A Van Life Day 169
- Chapter 25 179
  - Beyond Rejection 179
- Chapter 26 191
  - Heartbreak & Death - October 2019 ... 191
- Chapter 27 195
  - My online romance scammer 195
- Chapter 28 209
  - My Aura - Portugal December 2019 ... 209
- Chapter 29 213
  - Christmas in the UK 2019 213
- Chapter 30 217
  - Escape to Bali 217
- Chapter 31 237
  - Why do I need to feel loved? 237
- Chapter 32 241

My Corona Virus Birthday May 10th .. 241

Chapter 33 245

   Lock down Virtual Dating - May 2020 245

Chapter 34 251

   The Life I want to Live 251

Chapter 35 255

   And Now? 255

Chapter 36 259

   Escape to Portugal 259

Epilogue 263

   The Princess in her Ivory Tower 263

Chapter 1

Goodbye Conditioned Life - April 2019

As I walk around the house, seeing its emptiness, I no longer feel any attachment. All my life's belongings lovingly stowed away in boxes in the garage. I wonder if I will ever need them again. Just sixteen months ago I was so happy to be starting my life afresh. Moving into this lovely new home in the heart of the Sussex countryside, with its beautiful outlook over fields and the South Downs, with its awe-inspiring sunrises and sunsets. But after all the moving in was done, less than six months later, I was struck with the feeling that my life felt worthless. Yes, I had a nice home, a good job in Information Technology, wonderful friends, two amazing children, Georgina aged sixteen, Zachary aged thirteen and Rosie, our adorable chocolate Labrador. But despite this and having freedom every other weekend, when the children were with their Dad, to do whatever I pleased, still I couldn't shake off the feeling that there was meant to be more to my life than this.

Two days every two weeks, more than most people have, to spend time doing whatever makes you feel the happiest, really is no time at all when we have such a short time in this world. Maybe this feeling had come about as I had been working on improving my love for myself over the course of the months since moving in. I had enrolled in online courses for 'Becoming your best self'. Discovered Byron Katie 'Loving what is' and had been listening to spiritual leaders on YouTube, like Osho and Mooji and had started to meditate. I felt like a lost soul trying to find her way home.

At least now I was doing something about it, even if I didn't yet know where this would lead me. Telling friends and strangers about my plans seemed, in turn, to bring an open mindedness to them. People tell me I am brave, that I am inspiring following my dreams. I don't feel brave. I feel scared and of course excited, which is exactly how I should feel. I am taking a huge leap of faith in allowing life to guide me. I am trusting that the universe/God will take care of me. Travelling in a campervan was never actually a dream I remember having but now that is exactly what it feels like. A dream that is now going to be a reality.

Today is the first day of the rest of my life – Every day is this, it's just that we lose sight of it. If we could only be more conscious of this when we wake in the mornings, we would make the most of every day. Feel so much more alive, happier and grateful – just for our existence and another day's opportunity to relate with kindness and love to the rest of the world. The sun is shining, the birds are singing, the universe is happily sending me on my way.

Chapter 2
A Trip to Haiti - January 2017

For a long time, I'd had a hankering to volunteer on a project abroad helping to make a difference for communities in need. To feel that you have made even the smallest difference in people's lives seems to be a need for a lot of us. Although, now I have come to realise, you can make a difference everyday of your life offering the smallest of kindness to people. Even just a smile can change the course of someone's day.

So, when the opportunity came up in the Sussex village where I lived, to be part of a team going to 'Hope House Haiti', an orphanage and free school, I was only too happy to sign up. Because of my experience in amateur dramatics, I was allocated the task of directing the biblical show of 'Ruth', from the Book of Ruth. This is a love story, sparked between Ruth & Boaz, crossing cultural and forbidden love borders with real tragedy and heartache, but it does have a happy ending. It is also a story of a woman trusting in God and life for her very existence. It is set about 1150 BC, making this the oldest of all recorded love stories. I am a true romantic and a sucker for a love story.

We had ten days to put the show together. It was an incredulous feat by the whole team and the children, especially as they had never acted before. They had already learnt six songs in English but there were still lines to be learnt, fifty costumes to be made, and rehearsals to be taken with a Haitian interpreter. I have never been prouder of my endeavours than I was in that moment when the children took to the stage in front of their friends, families and local community. It felt like a miracle.

Dress rehearsal

Hope House is an incredible place full of the love and worship of God. It isn't really an orphanage but a beautiful big family.

Aside from the show, the team achieved so much despite mostly every one of us getting sick at some point with a forty-eight-hour stomach bug. Fortunately, I didn't get sick until after the show but it did mean that I missed out on the much-anticipated trip to the beach. The medical team gave health and sight check-ups to over five-hundred children who attend the free school. Religious music was recorded, and special evenings were organised. One night everyone dressed up in their finest dresses and we held a strictly ballroom competition. It was such a delight to see the children having so much fun.

One other highlight of the trip for me was when we took aid to an extremely poor village. I say highlight as it was a very humbling experience to see for myself what true poverty looks like. It was a little nerve racking as on our arrival there were men walking around carrying rifles. As the food was handed out from the back of the truck the villagers formed an orderly queue but it wasn't long before tensions started to rise. The order started to break down as the villagers pushed each other to get to the front and children were getting crushed. It was so sad to see the lack of care these people showed each other in the face of hunger. They were simply desperate and we had to leave before any trouble began.

One morning, as the sun was rising from behind the mountains, with the water from the lake glistening and reflecting its magnificence, I was sitting out on the balcony of the tree house like building we were sleeping in. A swift flew in my line of sight and then circled the trees in front of me, exactly three times, before vanishing as quickly as it had appeared. This struck me as significant as it was the only bird I had seen in the entire ten days I had been there.

This is what came into my mind in that very moment. "God gave birds wings to fly. Birds can fly many many miles over oceans to distant lands. It is not easy for them; they have to navigate many storms. God has given us wings too, wings in our hearts, so that we can fly ever closer to our Lord, even at times when we feel a storm is raging. Birds return home again and so we will always return to our Lord. A week and a half ago when I arrived in Haiti, I never thought God would have spoken to me. He gave me wings on a plane to fly to Haiti to find my way home." As I reflect on these words, the emotion I felt at the time returns to me. I am a Christian, baptised a Catholic, but I do not go to church very often. But I can honestly say that this was a profound spiritual moment for me.

Every morning at sunrise, around 5am, the family would come together for song and worship and I would always gratefully partake. That morning Yvrose, the founder of Hope House, and a truly inspirational woman, turned to me and said "Suzi, I think you have something that you would like to share". How did she know?!

There is more to this story... When the team first arrived at Hope House, we were welcomed by the children singing one of the songs that I had chosen for the show, 'Lean on Me' by Bill Withers. This was a very touching and emotional moment for me. Two weeks later at the airport on the way home, Leandra, our team leader, presented me with a can of coke from the airport shop with the song title, yes, you guessed it 'Lean on Me'.

This was my first awareness of signs from the universe. Now, some may say this was merely coincidence but even if it was, in my mind it could not be ignored. I am not a person who is easily able to ask for help. Not because I don't want it but because my life's experiences have made me very self-reliant.

One week after returning from Haiti I shared with Nick, my husband, that I could no longer stay in a marriage where I felt no love. A few months later I got myself a tattoo of a swift in an eternity loop with the words 'lean on me' on the inside of my wrist, lest I should ever forget to fly free. Being my truest self and never forgetting that I have God, the universe and friends to lean on. My book cover reflects this with the swift flying high and whenever I see these birds, usually at sunrise or sunset, I am always reminded.

Chapter 3

Meeting Ray - December 2017

Fifty-two years young, meeting Ray fifty-eight, from Malta, in the carpark of a rural village pub in the Hampshire countryside, on a cold but sunny Sunday in early December. My first date since separating ten months ago. I'm excited driving down the winding country roads from Sussex, no matter that it's going to take an hour and a half. Ray's tinder profile pictures were gorgeous. It's such a pleasurable journey with the mottled sun shining through the now bare branches of the trees.

I'm standing, in the carpark of the pub, in the middle of nowhere, waiting for my first glimpse of…here he comes, oh shit, he looks so old, nothing like his tinder picture. Never mind, let's just go with the flow. We greet with a gentle hug and I say in a girlish manner, apologetically "I'm not sure how I should be". What the f**k was that! I'm so nervous. He throws me completely by asking if I would like to go for a walk. I'm wearing brand new purple boots, not ideal for walking on muddy country lanes but I say "OK" and put on my jacket and scarf; it will be fine. Walking along desolate country lanes with a complete stranger! Not my brightest move, but he had taken me completely by surprise and I had not had time to think it through. We're chatting and after a few minutes he says he doesn't think he's going to be attracted to me in a romantic way. He is just reflecting my own feelings in that moment. I say I feel the same way, but this was not being very open minded of heart as how is it possible to know this after just a few minutes? Of course, there is always the immediate sixth sense intuition and chemistry at play but there is so much more to forming a deep, intimate connection than someone's physical appearance.

We walk for two hours, taking in everything, the beauty and tranquillity of the countryside, it's nice, even though now my new boots are caked in mud. When I take time to look at Ray, I see that beautiful face that was in the tinder picture, it's just his bohemian floppy hat that's hiding it. As we return, a few hundred yards from the pub carpark, the sun is now setting and clouds form a heart shape in the sky. We excitedly take photos; my fate is sealed in that moment.

Ray is walking behind me and he tells me that I look like a twenty-year-old from behind, and that he would like to make love to me. Caught off guard, once again, I quickly say "Well that's not going to happen". If I had known him then as I do now, I would have said "Thank you, that's a wonderful thing for you to have shared with me". It was a very vulnerable thing for him to do as he opened himself to total rejection. I tell him I never sleep with someone on a first date as then what is the draw to see me again! A rule I always had in my younger years; not much of a boundary to have! And there it was, I said yes, without actually saying it.

I see now my total lack of self-worth that I had for myself then and in my earlier years. That I thought the reason a man would desire to see me again would not be for who I was as a person but for 'sex'. And of course, if that was the energy I was vibrating then that's exactly what I would attract in and not the high value, emotionally available man who actually desired a relationship. You will see this playing out in subsequent chapters, as it was only much later on in my journey that I learnt I need to have boundaries in order to be with my truth of my values and maintain self-respect and love of myself.

In the pub, a very typical example of an English village drinking den with its wooden floorboards and memorabilia from bygone days, I order a small glass of Malbec so he doesn't think I am reckless (which of course is exactly what I can be), he has tea! He asks me if I would put my hand in his, I do, why not? Oh shit, I'm lost now, it feels perfect. We move to sit in front of the now roaring fire and suddenly two hours has gone by and I have no recollection of what we talked about. It's time for me to leave and go back to my current life, soon to be ex-husband, children Gina and Zach and Rosie dog. I'm still living in the family home whilst I wait for completion on my new house. It just seemed like the most natural thing to do as the way we were living was no different to how it had been for many years, together but apart. Very unconventional I know but it worked for us and I didn't want to waste money renting somewhere.

We're in the carpark and he's kissing me endlessly in the light of the full moon and my heart is on fire. We make no plans to see each other again and the moon shines its way for me along the country lanes. I stop on my way home to message "I loved you kissing me". He replied "Next time I'll give you a nice massage before kissing you! Then I'll kiss you all over your body!". Next time, what next time? He's flying home to Malta on Thursday. Then he messages "I thought about spending more time with you before I go back. 'Don't be without love so you won't feel dead. Die in love and stay alive forever'. 'Lovers don't finally meet somewhere. they're in each other all along' (Rumi)." I have died and gone to heaven!

Two days later and I'm picking Ray up at the airport to spend a night of love making. I'm completely crazy. He's postponed his flight until the following Tuesday, he's crazy too, well, that's what I thought at the time. I found this sweet little cottage immersed in the countryside not too far away from where I lived. The owner sells second hand books so there are numerous shelves laden with them throughout the cottage. Ray happens to love old books so he is in his element. There is a log fire, one of the reasons I chose this particular cottage as I love an open fire. Something we had in the family house as I was growing up. I remember sitting endlessly in front of it watching the dance of the flames and feeling happy and content in its warmth. It was only normally alight when my Dad was at home at the weekends. It was the first thing we did on arrival; Ray lit the fire while I poured two glasses of champagne. I certainly needed it for some 'Dutch courage'. I shyly undress, in preparation for the massage that Ray is going to honour me with. This was the first time in seventeen years a man, other than my husband, had seen my naked body. Of course, I felt very conscious about how I looked and I wasn't as confident about my body as I am now. I actually have a beautiful body, especially for a woman of my age, definitely not perfect, but whose is? It's simply knowing how to love, accept and embrace our own bodies exactly as they are. That's what gives us the confidence to be our true selves, when we are not hung up on what anyone else thinks.

I lay naked, on the soft fleece blanket I had brought with me, in front of the crackling fire and Ray gives me the most incredible massage. After many years of having no touch this was just how I had dreamt it would be. Every sinew in my body was being ignited and my senses were overloaded. I could feel the softness of the blanket beneath me, the warmth of the fire, and the caressing touch of Ray's hands on my body. I was in heaven.

There was no rushing and it was not until a couple of hours later that we ascended the stairs to the bedroom. I cannot say how long or how many times we made love that night but it was a few.

Despite having to go to work the next morning, a drive to Kent around the M25 motorway, I did so with such an enormous smile on my face and love in my heart. We had decided to stay another night so Ray spent the day exploring the countryside until I returned in the evening after collecting the children from school and taking them home. Responsibilities could not be abandoned. Another evening of love making ensued. I was insatiable. Ray was the perfect person to arouse me from my slumber, with his loving touch and sensitivity.

The following day was Saturday and we sadly had to leave the cottage as it was already booked out for the weekend. I found us alternative lodgings at a local bed and breakfast, albeit a very nice one. That evening Ray treated me to a lovely meal out at the local pub and I was surprised not to see anyone I knew. Once again, a night of love making ensued. In the morning we sat in front of yet another pub fire, which Ray had made up, and enjoyed a hearty breakfast. It was raining so we stayed for most of the day, just embracing the ambience of the pub with its warming fire, until it was time to leave for our final night together. I had found an old ferry boat down in

Shoreham harbour, a place where there is a community of house boats, each one unique in its own way reflecting the character of its owner. It was a lovely boat with a woodburning stove and a captain's quarters downstairs where we slept. It even had a writing desk which Ray utilised to write his journal. In the dark of the late afternoon, we went for a stroll, hand in hand, around the town and on to the beach, where we kissed with the gentle sound of the waves washing over the pebbles. Returning to the houseboat Ray cooked a lovely warming soup. I do love a man that cooks because it's not one of my favourite past times, although, when I put my mind to it, I'm actually quite a good cook. That evening was to be our last of lovemaking, and the following morning when I dropped him off at Gatwick airport there was a sadness in my heart, but I was so grateful for the love that he had shared with me.

Chapter 4

New Beginnings

On the 16th December I moved into my new house in Henfield, a small village in West Sussex at the foot of the South Downs, with stunning views over the countryside. The only piece of furniture I owned was a sofa as I was buying everything new for a fresh start, but I didn't care. I was just so happy to have my own home. The week that followed, leading up to Christmas, was completely chaotic with deliveries of furniture and white goods arriving every day. I was determined to have everything in situ by Christmas Eve, including a real Christmas tree, for when the children were going to be spending their first night with me. This meant lots of late nights trying not to get frustrated with assembling beds, wardrobes and a kitchen table and chairs. Flat packed furniture is not designed to be done by one person and I ended up with so many bruises.

But I did it, and we all had comfy beds to sleep in Christmas Eve night when Santa came as usual to deliver stockings overflowing with presents. This year I wanted to overly spoil the children. Something I always try not to do, so as not to ruin their appreciation of what they do receive, something I learnt from my parents and I have always been very appreciative of this life lesson. I probably wanted to spoil them now just because I could, and no longer had to ask a husband's permission. So, they both got a gaming laptop and of course they were delighted. I felt like a good mum that day, not allowing the guilt I felt at splitting up the family to take hold. Of course, being frivolous helped to allay some of that guilt.

I dropped the children off back at the family home to have Christmas lunch with their Dad, Grandma and Grandad. Little did we know that this was to be the last Christmas that they would all have together as their Grandad died the following June. I spent my first Christmas, since leaving home in my early twenties, with my Mum, Dad, sister and brother. It was actually really very nice and for the first Christmas in a long time I didn't get drunk, mainly because I was driving home afterwards. Christmas Day had always been challenging with my mother and father-in-law and I think a lot of people resort to drinking their way through the day.

On December 27th I flew to Malta to spend four days with Ray.

I remember sitting on the floor of his apartment, cross legged, surrounded by his artwork and sculptures, in front of the floor to ceiling windows gazing at the view of the sea with its white horses. I wanted to stay there forever, but of course it was not possible. I was so in the moment with him but was acutely aware that I had opened my heart knowing that I would likely suffer pain on losing him but he had given me hope that I could love again. Every single moment was so precious, when we made love and even when we touched, I felt a part of him it made my heart bleed. I often cried during our love making, it was so deeply emotional. I'm not sure if it was because I had deprived myself of such affection for so long or because it was a truly special connection. Some of both I think.

Climbing down a cliff at Siggiewi

It was a beautiful time and of course I was becoming more attached. Ray noticed this and mentioned he was worried about my expectations. But how could I realistically have any expectations, he lived in Malta with very few commitments and I in England with tons of responsibilities. I was very emotionally vulnerable but had learnt how being in the moment, present, means you can experience everything with full awareness. What was the worst that could happen? I would have some amazing memories and know that my life's course had been changed.

I am remembering how envious I was of Ray's life in Malta. He manages a couple of Airbnb apartments, belonging to his family and helps out on a friend's farm. But his true calling is as an artist, he paints and sculpts. A pretty simple unconditioned life. I had just committed myself to a mortgage and bills. In that moment a seed was sown in my mind that I was not even conscious of.

When he dropped me at the airport, he said he definitely wanted to do a sculpture of me, and would come to England, maybe at the end of January. A couple of days earlier I had asked if I could commission him to make a nude sculpture of me after I had seen the ones he had made of the *'fat lady of Malta'*. I thought it would be fun to experience and nice to have, now I was embracing my inner goddess.

Chapter 5

The love story continues - Jan 2018

So true to his word, Ray arrived in England late January enroute to see his parents in Canada. His dad wasn't well and had asked him to visit.

At this time, I had started an online course 'How to become the most attractive version of yourself' by Shelley Bullard, a love coach. We attract people and experiences into our lives, whether we realise it or not, based on how we feel inside about these things. We want to be able to attract the things that allow us to feel really good and enable us to live a fulfilled and truly happy life. We attract partners who mirror what we believe about relationships on the inside. We attract money (or not) based on how we identify with money and wealth on the inside. And we attract life experiences that mirror who we are and what we believe. You will see from the following chapters that learning to love myself in the way that I want others to love me has been challenging. Every time I thought I had it mastered, I would recognise that there was more inner work to be done. Now I am enlightened in knowing that this is lifelong work. There is always room for self-growth.

Ray's visit was fleeting, he flew to Canada three days later. But it gave us some quality time together. He introduced me to the teachings of a man called Paul Lowe, a consciousness guru, whom he had met at a retreat many years ago. He talks about being fully conscious in the moment, there only being the here and now. He also doesn't believe in a totally monogamous relationship, that if you meet someone, irrespective of whether you have a partner, if you are truly being present then you will just be in the moment with your feelings. If you desire to have intimacy with them then that is what you should flow with. But also, to be honest and open about it with your partner as this will lead to a more deepening connection. This is how Ray feels. My argument about this is that if you are truly happy and fulfilled with your partner why would you even have a desire to be intimate with someone else. I know this is how I feel when I am relating intimately with a man. Maybe the point is that you shouldn't limit yourself as the intimacy you share with different people is always special and unique.

Meeting Ray set me on my spiritual path of becoming a more conscious and mindful person in all aspects of my life. I was hungry for knowledge and understanding.

Of course, once Ray left for Canada, I was fearful to hear from him that maybe he had met someone there. This would take our relating to a whole new level completely and would show me whether I was capable of having an unconditional conscious love relationship with him. Well, two days before he was due back in England, actually on Valentine's day, he told me that he had kissed someone that day and she was going to visit him in Malta. I briefly felt pain and then anger but I seemed to transition out of it pretty quickly by not allowing my thoughts to make a story. To put all this into perspective, in the morning Ray had sent me a Happy Valentines message and later on the Rumi quote that he had sent me the night after we first met 'Lovers don't finally meet somewhere, they are in each other all along'. I adore Rumi's quotes. And in the evening 'Out beyond ideas of wrong doing and right doing there is a field. I'll meet you there. When the soul lies down in that grass the world is too full to talk about'. It was just a kiss and maybe she will never go to Malta. And even if she did, it's nothing to do with my relating with Ray. I want it to be of no consequence to me. It has reminded me that I must live my own life and not revolve any of it around him. Something I need to be aware of when I am relating with any man, as this is a tendency of mine. And it is something that can repel an emotionally available man. It is so important for a healthy relationship to make space for your own life while moving forward together in a relationship. I need to be in my own life.

I am maybe going to be out of my depth with this conscious relating and unconditional love stuff but it's all within my control to stop at any time I choose. I was just scared. Scared of getting hurt. I was determined that when Ray returned, I would make the most of every moment he was with me knowing that it may be our last time together.

Making love on his return was simply amazing, we spent the whole day in bed and I was completely satiated. In the afterglow of lovemaking, we shared some thought-provoking childhood memories. It is unresolved wounding from childhood that we carry with us throughout life that causes us to act out unhealthy patterns in our lives. This is where are fears rise from. Understanding these wounds is imperative to living our best and happiest life. I often find, in the afterglow of sex, this the perfect time for sharing your most vulnerable self which always brings a deeper connection. In that moment I felt so happy, heard and seen

Ray introduced me to 'Loving What is' by Byron Katie. I really resonate with what she says. We can only ever believe the reality of a situation as this is the truth and if our thoughts are with anything different, we are believing a lie and this is what causes us the pain. She explains how to do the 'work' on anything that you believe, past or present that causes you emotional pain. This has really helped me to navigate my feelings better especially in times when I have felt lost. Her work helps to let go of the story and be happy in the reality and truth.

When Ray first told me that he wasn't feeling horny towards me and then a day or so later that he lacked the desire to kiss me, I had an opportunity to put into practise what I had been learning from Byron Katie. It was all down to me, having thoughts that this could be our last time together, and he was just mirroring what I was projecting. That night I told him I didn't want sex as kissing was an important intimacy to me. I was setting my boundary for my desires and I felt empowered. Then he wanted to make love and kissed me and we were both just present in the moment.

The next morning, he started on the sculpture of me, it looked great, he has a real talent. I was feeling very aroused lying on the sofa naked and Ray did admit to me later in the day he had felt horny but at the time he was focussed on the task. That evening he gave me the most incredible back massage and I even fell asleep on the floor in the living room, I was so relaxed and at peace with myself.

The following night, very spontaneously, I booked a flight to Sicily to trek Mount Etna! It was something that Ray had been talking to me about doing and I decided in that moment I would really like to do it, so in the vein of not revolving my life around him, I took my first steps. In the morning, I told him, he thought it was cool. I loved the feeling of being in control of my own destiny.

I notice that in times of emotional upset I make spontaneous decisions for plans for something exciting to look forward to. I guess this is my coping mechanism but also a way to bring pleasure and joy back into my life.

Our final night together Ray cooked a lovely meal and told me about his day in Brighton. He had bought me presents, some red leather gloves, that I have in the van and have been so great to wear driving when it's been cold and a beautiful purple scarf from India. He also showed me how to do some clay modelling and made a fun quick piece of himself. At 9.30pm once again he surprised me by asking "Shall we go to bed?" We lay snuggled up against each other and I stroked his back for a long time and eventually we naturally fell asleep. Later I was awoken at 5am by him stroking my leg. In my dreamy state I asked him to lick my pussy, asking for my desire without fear of rejection, yes! He gladly obliged and then we made love. It was perfect and we rested well until morning came.

In the kitchen, as I went to move the plastic container with the clay in it from the window ledge, behind it I noticed a card for me. I left it where it was as I obviously wasn't supposed to have found it just yet! When I dropped him at the airport he said "I'll see you at Gatwick, Sicily, Malta or Morocco." I replied "Who knows" and indeed this was the truth.

As soon as I got back home, I opened the card. It read 'Thank you for being my *"Loving what is"* Partner, Lots of Love, Ray'. The card itself had hearts on it, it was so beautiful; I was not used to such thoughtfulness and love.

Four days after Ray returned to Malta he asked if he could come with me to Mt. Etna. Of course, I was so happy that he wanted to share this adventure with me.

Chapter 6
Mt. Etna Sicily - April 2018

As I sat at the airport waiting for the gate number of my flight to Catania, I was excited but nervous. Nervous for trekking up Mt. Etna, a live volcano, and nervous for camping out in the cold temperatures. I had read that it could drop to as low as minus ten degrees Celsius, depending on how high up you were, but I had invested in a good sleeping bag. Nervous for seeing Ray because of uncertainty of his current feelings of desire for me. I know I can only *'Love what is'*.

Sometimes I am unsure how I feel towards Ray knowing that he won't be monogamous with me. For now, I just want to be in the moment and once I am with him, I will be. I want to be my most authentic self. I have nothing to fear as I feel the best I ever have about myself. I feel I know who I am as a person although my true self is still evolving. Whatever, experiences were to come in the following days would be perfect as I would just be *'Loving what is'*. Bring it on!

I was so excited to see Mt. Etna when the plane landed with its beautiful snow-capped peak. I couldn't wait to be immersed in and feel at one with nature as this is where I always feel grounded and at peace with myself.

Half an hour after coming through arrivals expecting to see Ray waiting, I eventually found him. He had wandered off to get a cup of coffee. There was a point I wondered whether he was going to be there and I was starting to feel anxious. How was I going to find my way to Catania? He greeted me with a gentle hug and we walked outside and there waiting was the bus. Easy enough, but I would never have worked out where to get off if Ray hadn't been with me. Half an hour later we arrived and found our accommodation where we would spend the night before catching the early morning bus up to Mt. Etna. It was nothing special, just somewhere to sleep. We both had showers and after five weeks of not seeing each other I assumed we would be making love. But Ray seemed exhausted and was laying on the bed with his eyes closed. I stroked his back for a long while but it was evident that nothing was going to happen that night. I should have said something but I was fearful of his response. My intuition was telling me something that I wanted to ignore. I hardly slept wondering and it was so noisy in the building, the walls seemed to be paper thin.

Ray didn't want to get up early to get the bus so he had arranged with someone he knew to give us a lift later in the day which gave us time for him to show me around Catania. It is very pretty and historic and I actually stood in the stunning setting of the photo I had seen on the internet in the main square, surrounded by historical buildings with Mt. Etna's imposing peak rising up from behind.

Late afternoon we got our ride up to the start of the Altomontana path on the south side of Mt. Etna. The road climbs up and around for what felt an eternity. We found the start of the path and walked through sweet-smelling pine forests which opened out onto the rugged lava slopes. The further and higher we climbed the more snow lay on the path and as we walked, we passed a few people returning from their day out. Dusk was falling and we needed to get to the first refugio, although we had no idea whether it would be open or not. There are a number of refugios, stone huts with a wooden roof and big fireplaces along the 37km trail going from the south of Mt. Etna to the north. Finally, as the sun was setting magnificently over Sicily, we reached the refugio San Galverina with the imposing peak of Mt.

Etna smoking right behind us. It felt like we were on top of the world.

San Galverina refugio

We were both so happy when we found it open and the fire was even alight. There was stale bread, wine and beer that had been left by previous visitors which felt like a gift. I named it the best hotel in the world. It really is the simplest things in life that bring the most pleasure. It has the most amazing view over Sicily, a huge fire place, (and you know how much I love those) a wood store, a water tap and it was free. It was so amazing to fall asleep next to a huge crackling fire.

As the next morning dawned, I awoke early with the sun rising and tended the fire until it was roaring again whilst Ray slept on. I still hadn't even had a kiss from him. The closest we had been to any kind of intimacy was when I was laying on the bed in the hotel in the morning and he had stroked my back. I mentioned to him on the way up that he didn't seem very happy, as he was being very quiet, but he said he was just meditating as he was walking as his boots were tight. Well, he didn't take that moment to tell me how he was feeling towards me. So that morning I was feeling sad as I just didn't understand why he was not being intimate and I was still too fearful to ask. I just kept hoping that some intimacy would happen. Having separate sleeping areas didn't help, as there were two separate stone benches to lay on but not large enough to accommodate two people side by side.

Ray spent most of the first day laying in the sun on the side of Mt. Etna. His neck and knees were hurting from carrying his back pack so I went for an exploration walk down the trail opposite the refugio. It was all downhill and the further I went the snow depth increased which made it very hard to walk in as my boots kept sinking into it. After forty-five minutes of this struggle, I thought it best to turn back especially as Ray didn't even know I had gone. A few people stopped by the refugio that day and one couple gave us chocolate cupcakes. It felt like we were being provided for. We had only brought a basic food supply with us, just enough for the four days, so we were grateful for anything extra anyone gave us.

The same thing happened the next day when three Italian men visited. I say visit because Ray and I had made ourselves quite at home. They gave us a salami and cheese roll, tea and a shot of some homemade brew. It all tasted so good because, of course, we appreciate things so much more when there is not an abundance.

Then finally, some intimacy. Ray suggested that we wash each other's feet! An unusual suggestion but it was glorious with warm water heated up over the fire. Later I offered to massage some deep heat into his shoulder which turned into a full-blown massage with him lying on his bed with me straddled across him. In the midst of this a French couple arrived so I had to jump off as it was rather a compromising position, although I was fully clothed. I'm sure they thought they had interrupted us, well they had. Although, I don't think the intimacy would have gone beyond the massage, no matter how much I would have liked it to have.

The French couple stayed for a while and we exchanged oil and bread for a cup of tea and turmeric. I loved that we shared in this way. Life was truly providing for us.

Eventually, Ray and I went for a walk together although we weren't gone for long as there was too much snow on the track. It really was a little too early in the season to properly trek. Skis would have been fun and indeed one day a skier came down the side of the volcano behind us.

However, we returned at the end of May and trekked the entire trail from the North to the South.

Our final evening together we exchanged massages in front of the fire, albeit sitting and with our clothes on. We both went to bed feeling very relaxed and Ray gave me a warm hug to thank me and just before I got into bed he reached for my hand and said goodnight. A beautiful moment. Sadly, this intimacy was to be short lived. In the morning when I went over to him to obviously give him a kiss, he turned his head away so I ended up just hugging him instead. As I looked up two small birds flew by reminding me to *'fly free'*. Ray and I had no future in a romantic relationship together and only when I truly accepted this would the pain for me stop. In that moment I decided just to be present with enjoying our last day together in the incredible place that Mt. Etna is. The sun was shining and all felt right.

I sat reflecting on the way that Ray engages with people and notice how it brings joy into their lives in that moment he connects with them. He shows real interest and is not superficial, as most of us often are, when we meet or talk to strangers. I've been trying to be more like that in my everyday life, but it's still something I have to do consciously but it appears to come to Ray so naturally and he really takes time to hear the person he is engaging with. This is part of relating consciously towards people.

As we walked back down Mt. Etna Ray was being exceptionally chatty, which I noticed I really liked, but then the bombshell came. He asked "How do I feel about us not making love", and there it was. I told him that I still wanted to make love with him but had been sensing he didn't desire to with me. He said that it often happens to him with a woman that he suddenly stops wanting to have sexual intimacy but couldn't explain why. As we continued to walk, I let my tears fall. We got to the end of the trail and hitched a ride (a first for me) back down to the town of Nicollosi where Ray bought me a large glass of red wine to enjoy in the sun whilst he disappeared off to look at hiking boots. Later we caught the bus back to Catania and found our room for the night which, thankfully, was very nice.

I cried during the night; I don't know if Ray even realised. I so didn't want to be close to him, I just wanted to run. Run from facing the feeling of pain that was engulfing me. I don't think he had any idea of how sad I was feeling. In the morning I packed my bag and told him I was leaving, that I wanted to walk and be on my own. He didn't know what to say. We hugged, he kissed me on the lips and I left. Not much of a parting after all we had shared. He seemed pained. I found a place on the steps of the cathedral to sit in full view of Mt. Etna as I had time to kill before I needed to get the bus back to the airport. All I wanted to do was cry, let the emotion flow out, but I was holding it all in because I was in a public place.

I had made plans to stop off in Malta to spend a couple of days with a friend before heading back to England. Some girl time was just what I needed and it was here, whilst sunbathing on her balcony, that the thought came to me about buying a campervan. Ray had shared with me previously that he had a dream of travelling in a van. Out of the ashes rises a Phoenix.

Before I left Malta, I decided to see Ray, to face my fear of rejection. His flight back from Catania wasn't arriving until late afternoon so I had a lovely lunch with my friend overlooking Spinola Bay and then headed off to visit Hagar Qim temple; a megalithic complex among the most ancient religious sites on earth, perched on the cliffs overlooking the Mediterranean Sea. It was the perfect way to spend the afternoon and I was definitely in the right vibration when we met.

He took me to his secret garden on the cliffs where there was the most beautiful sunset and, on the way back, we sat overlooking the sea for a little while.

Ray's secret garden

As we got up to leave, he asked me if I would like a hug. Of course I would and I felt a real sense of love and connection. Ray's hugs are gentle and last for minutes. We should all take more time to linger in a hug, they are so good for the soul. We ended up in the 'farmers bar', which I loved as it's a place where the local men hang out playing cards. We ate tuna sandwiches and I had a glass of wine and conversation flowed easily. I dropped him back to the farm and we hugged and he kissed me gently on the lips. I wasn't sad.

Chapter 7

The Van

It wasn't long after returning home from Malta that I began watching YouTube videos on van life. The more I watched the more I was convinced that this was a life I wanted to experience, at least for a year. Waking up and going to sleep surrounded by nature, living a simple small footprint life and with ultimate freedom.

I started to research into the cost of new and second-hand vans. It just so happened that very near to where I lived was a company that buys new vans and converts them into campervans. They were pretty expensive, ranging from £35K to £50K. But I knew as soon as I saw them, I was going to buy one. I wanted to feel secure, as far as possible, that I wouldn't be having any breakdown issues.

My first challenge was to work out how I would be able to finance it. As I had paid off all my credit card debt from my separation alimony, I was actually in a very viable financial position to get a loan. I just needed to ensure that I had enough money saved to make the repayments each month and then at the end of the year I would be able to sell the van and repay the outstanding loan. Well, that was the plan.

The following week I returned and put down the £1000 non-refundable deposit for one Nissan NV300 campervan, which came with a five-year return to base warranty from anywhere in Europe. Now all I had to do was wait six months, which actually turned into eight as the van didn't arrive in the UK from the factory until the following January. But this gave me all the time I needed to plan my exit from work (I was on a three-month notice contract), try to save as much money as possible, explain to my family and rent the house out.

I finally had a plan for my life that filled me with hope and excitement. Just knowing that I would be leaving gave me a new appreciation of everything my life currently was. I wanted to make the most of every second of it because one thing I knew, that whatever happened, I wouldn't be coming back to the same life.

Chapter 8
A Tinder Date - July 2018

After five months of being upset over Ray I finally felt ready to have another date. I think it took me so long to be able to move on as he was, after all, my first lover for seventeen years. I needed time to allow all my blocked love to flow freely, which manifested itself as heartache and tears. I read recently that grief is love with nowhere to go. This made so much sense to me.

I did wonder whether it was a good idea to date as I didn't want to become too attached to anyone, only to have to leave them. But I felt a need to feel love from a man and share intimacy.

I met with Raimon outside Brighton station on what was forecast as a wet and windy day. It's OK to laugh at his name, I still do, and it was a great source of entertainment for my friends for a long time that I chose to date someone with such a similar name to Ray. In fact, I think it still is. I didn't instantly find Raimon attractive, but he had a cuteness about him and I loved that he wanted to put his arm around me walking down the street when we had only just met. Raimon is from Catalonia and I have come to learn that most West European men are a lot more relaxed about being tactile on a first date, then British men. We went for a drink first, I definitely needed one to calm my nerves. But it turned out not to be so necessary as we had such an easy-going conversation getting to know each other.

As it had started to rain, we headed to Brighton museum and stopped in the entrance of the Pavilion. Raimon took me by surprise by giving me the most gloriously passionate long snog. I really loved that. It's always good to get that first kiss out of the way. I find there is such expectation as the way someone kisses you can make or break the connection, more so for a woman, I think. A kiss is a conversation without words that conveys so much. Now the ice was broken, we had such fun in the museum and Raimon kept wanting to kiss me, a sign that he was definitely into me. Afterwards we headed down to Brighton seafront to watch the rough sea and he was keen to take photos of me, unusual for a first date I thought. We both love this photograph, although this was the last-time I put makeup on for a date. I don't generally wear makeup in everyday life so I feel I should not portray something I am not, even for a date. I am enough in my natural glory.

Then it was time for me to head home so we kissed goodbye at Brighton station with a date lined up for the following Sunday. I was a little unsure whether I was attracted enough to want to have sex with Raimon but I was happy to stay open and meet again and see how I felt.

So, the following Sunday we met on Hove seafront on a gloriously hot summer's day. We ate bread and cheese that I had brought with me and drank pear cider. We frolicked in the sea together and were like a couple of teenagers misbehaving on the beach. Raimon couldn't keep his eyes or hands off me. I loved it. Finally, I was one of those couples that I have looked at in envy. We left as the sun was going down with a chill in the air and I drove us back to

Raimon's flat. Once there all the foreplay of the afternoon on the beach culminated into long and blissful lovemaking. If I had doubts as to my attraction to Raimon they were now banished.

One evening, a couple of weeks into our relating, when we were out walking on the seafront watching the sunset, Raimon told me he was exclusive with me. I remember the feeling of fear that rose in me. I hadn't been looking for a serious relationship as after all next year I was off travelling the world in my van. But that was still eight months away, anything could happen in that time. When I'm in a sexual relationship with a man I do not want to be having sex with anyone else. In fact, I don't even desire to, but I understand that when you first meet someone nowadays mostly the 'rules', if you can call them that, are not the same as they were when I was in my thirties. Everyone is a lot more relaxed about having sex with other people whilst you are still getting to know someone. But call me old school but that is not for me.

But, neither Raimon nor I like to use a condom so I was happy for us to be exclusive. I know this maybe too much information for some but I mention it because I am sure there will be people reading this that maybe in the same situation. It seems that most men and women would rather not use one. You just have to do what's right for you. Remember it's always your choice.

Our relationship was everything I desired, fun, affectionate and passionate. We rode this wave for the entire month of August until I voiced my desire for our relationship. We often fear telling someone our true thoughts or feelings in case the outcome is not what we hoped for, and unfortunately this is exactly what happened. However, if you don't communicate your feelings you will never experience true connection. You will only create the relationship you want by being courageous enough to hear no.

At the end of August Raimon was headed back to his home town in Catalonia for a week. Everything was blissful between us. He had even said that he would maybe like to go to Scotland with me at Christmas for a few days. I was excited at the prospect and that he was wanting to make future plans. Always a good sign. When he returned after his week away, we were so happy to see each other, and it was shortly after that I revealed my truth one evening when we were messaging amorously. I asked whether we were still just dating or whether he considered me to be his girlfriend. Maybe I intuitively sensed something as he then told me he had kissed someone when he was away. I was hurt that he hadn't told me when I had seen him as my belief is you need absolute trust to have a successful relationship. I wasn't cross about the kiss as he was just being in the moment. He told me he was going to tell me but he was scared to because he didn't want to hurt me. Well, that had worked out well then. But then he delivered the bombshell that he didn't want to be so serious and might want to meet with other women. I didn't think we were serious, just enjoying each other's company, but for him he felt that I was serious because I wanted to see him on a regular basis. I wanted to be exclusive and it appeared he no longer did. I see now that I was not being in my feminine energy here, I was not leaning back in the relationship to allow him to pursue me. Apparently, I was his priority though! Interpret that how you will.

I know that when he first told me he felt he may meet with other women I should have walked away, honoured myself and my boundaries. He was revealing his truth and I should have listened. But I had been prepared to have an open relationship with Ray so why not just stay open and see what evolved. I guess the inevitable happened!

We continued to see each other as if nothing had been said, had lovely dates and amazing sex and two weeks later I flew to India with Ray for a ten-day tantra retreat at Osho Nisarga in Dharamshala, India. Something I had booked for us before I had met

Raimon hoping that it would bring a deeper connection to our relationship.

Chapter 9

Osho Nisarga Tantra Retreat India - September 2018

I organised this retreat with Ray to experience what real Tantra is, on my mission to truly understand spiritual love and learn how to open myself fully to my sexuality. When you say the word *'tantra'* most people will instantly think of sex but it is so much more than this. It is a conscious connection to sexuality, love and spirituality that liberates our minds, heart and soul.

After twenty-four hours we finally arrived at Osho Nisarga in Dharamshala at 9am. We had a six-hour night time layover at Delhi airport which wasn't much fun as there were no empty seats to sit on in the main terminal and we couldn't go through security to the departures hall until we had checked in our bags two hours before flight departure. You weren't even allowed outside of the building. However, the flight from London to Delhi had been great, we had a row of seats each as the flight was less than half full and we managed to get a good few hours of sleep. The flight from Delhi to Dharamshala was the smallest plane I've ever been on, just fifty seats and with propellers. I felt the fear as I walked across the runway to board, but actually it was a surprisingly smooth journey as it was such a lovely sunny day. The view of the Himalayas as we came into land was so incredible.

Dharamshala airport

After a crazy taxi ride, my first experience of roads in India, with people, dogs and various other animals wandering along both sides of the road, all with a seemingly sense of purpose, we arrived at the sanctuary that is Osho Nisarga. We had a beautiful river side cottage on stilts with a view of the snow-capped Himalayas. I had to pinch myself to know that I was really there.

View from the cottage – The Himalayas

Ma Ananda Sarita is a world renowned tantra master and mystic and she did not disappoint. To be honest I was completely in awe of her and this experience was to turn into a rollercoaster ride of emotions for me. The retreat revolves around a third of the 112 tantra meditation sutras. Each year one third is covered so you can return and have a whole unique experience. The meditation card I picked was perfect for me and it was one of the meditations that we would be doing. 'Beloved, at this moment let mind, knowing, breath, form, be included' I had no idea at that point how perfect a meditation this was going to be for me.

Osho

The retreat was to begin at 6pm with what is called the Osho White Robe Meditation where everyone wears a white robe and I felt like a goddess wearing mine. I was a little apprehensive but this came to be one of my favourite parts of the day. You start off with slow solo dancing/movement in your space which gradually becomes more energetic as does the music. This goes on for about twenty minutes and is then followed by listening to a discourse from Osho followed by silent meditation.

The daily schedule was full on and we were expected to attend all sessions to get the most out of the retreat experience. Each day started at 6.30am with Osho Dynamic Meditation. This meditation is a fast, intense and thorough way to break old, ingrained patterns in the body mind that keep one imprisoned in the past and to experience the freedom, the witnessing, silence and peace that are hidden behind those prison walls. However, this needs to be done for a minimum of twenty-one days in a row to be able to experience the full intention. It wasn't my favourite thing as it was very physically demanding as well as uncomfortable in what was required, but I guess this is the whole point of it. I must admit I skipped quite a few of these sessions.

Meditation Sanctuary

Daily Schedule

8.00 to 9.00 silent meditation by the river followed by the silent zen meditation walk

9.15 Breakfast

10.30-13.00 Session One

13.00-13.45 Lunch, time to rest

15.00–17.00 Session Two

17.00-17.20 Tea break, time for a quick shower as often the afternoon activities would leave you dripping in sweat

18.00-19.00 White Robe Brotherhood

19.30–20.15 dinner

21.00–22.30 Session Three

Phew, I'm exhausted just remembering. At the end of the day, I would fall into bed exhausted but with love in my heart and a smile on my face. The meditations included breath work, various types of massage (healing and cleansing), painting, many blindfolded activities, silent meditation, sound meditation, dancing, a lot of dancing and role playing.

Sarita encouraged us to connect with anyone we felt an attraction for and would like to spend time with. There was a number of good-looking younger men but my mind was stuck on Raimon. This was also going to be an interesting time for my relationship with Ray.

Day One was focussed on love and relating, lots of eye contact practices, hugging and dancing. What better way to start to let go of any inhibitions? This was followed by what turned out to be a very emotional role play. My choice was centred around the thought of not feeling loved and abandonment, something so many of us struggle with. I felt so connected with my partner in that moment. Often it is easier to share with a complete stranger your deepest fears and desires and we both shed tears. The evening session was massage, naked if you wanted, I didn't. I had taken the opportunity over lunch to ask the only Englishman if he would be my partner that evening. It was a safe choice for me! This wasn't always going to be the case as often the choice was not our own.

We formed pods of eight people and at the end of the day we came together to discuss how the day had unfolded for each of us and anything that may have arisen from it. This ended with a five-minute group snuggle. Amazing to be cuddled by multiple people at the same time.

Day Two was painting an object's energy, a game of consciousness and sixth sense and sound meditation after which we were put into a vow of silence until lunchtime the following day. I actually really loved this space. Ray spent the evening out, until late, with an Indian lady that he had done massage with so was not embracing the vow of silence. Having someone that you have shared intimacy with in the past and letting go of any jealousy I found was painful. This was just because of my thoughts of rejection. But he was not rejecting me in that moment, he'd already done that back in March on our trip to Mt. Etna. So, this time was good for me to practise just being with that feeling, noticing it and letting it go.

I had been feeling really tired and was experiencing back and neck pain, partly due to the physical demands my body was suddenly being put under and partly caused by the emotional unblocking that had begun to take place. My stomach hadn't been good since we arrived, due to the complete overnight change to a nutritious vegan Indian diet.

Day Three and the evening session was the meditation from the card I blindly chose on Day One. 'Beloved, at this moment let mind, knowing, breath, form, be included'. This meditation relates to the seven chakras. We danced in the feel of every single one of them. It started off quite sensually but gradually turned into an orgy of dance, (with clothes), although a lot of the younger Indian men did take off their tops. Everyone was sweating profusely but it was so much fun. Ray missed all of this as he didn't come to any of the sessions that day.

Day Four was all about Purification & Healing. We did a really beautiful sensual meditation today which I shared with an older sexy Indian man with beautiful long hair. Ray was now sick with a bug that seemed to be going around with the men and he never made it back to any of the sessions. I was happy that the Indian lady he had been spending time with was taking care of him as it meant I was able to fully participate still without the added concern of attending his needs. Don't get me wrong, I did make sure he had everything he required but I wasn't going to run around after him. During this period, I became friends with the Indian woman and we are still in contact today and I have an open invite to visit her in Delhi.

Day Five was a very emotionally traumatic day for me. The morning session was to dance for forty minutes as if making love to the universe, really slow sensual movements with no inhibition. About twenty minutes in I started crying, but I continued to dance. When the dancing ended, we did a prayer to the universe five times, on our knees with arms raised high. This created a body like orgasm, shaking and some people were even moaning. It was crazy stuff and after the third time of raising my arms I just started sobbing uncontrollably. I couldn't stop and it felt like an incredible release of emotion. Afterwards it was explained to me as my chakra channels opening allowing past blocks to leave my body, a type of purging ritual if you like. I look back on this as a very defining moment of my heart opening. In that moment I made myself completely vulnerable.

Day Six was a day of interesting sessions. Going beyond the form of outside appearance which meant 'acting out sex' with someone we didn't necessarily find attractive. A lot of people had already coupled up so were partnered with someone they were already in connection with, attracted to, so of course it was easier for them. I was paired with an older lovely Canadian man, with a big bushy beard, and I was in no way attracted to him. I was unable to go beyond the form and kiss or get sexual with him. Instead, we had an open discussion about it and he completely understood. I was happy that I was not scared to set boundaries. However, we did then alternate men and I ended up having a very hot sexy close contact dance with one of the younger Indian men.

The last session was 'near death experience'. I really didn't enjoy this. Starving your body of oxygen is not a great feeling. It wasn't just holding your breath but your nose also and with plugs in your ears. I know for some people asphyxiation heightens the enjoyment of sex but for me I just felt like I was suffocating. We were fully in control of our bodies but were encouraged to not stop. I was relieved when it was all over.

That evening was the naming ceremony for those who wanted to join the Osho family. A crazy wild celebration of dance and connection. I chose not to join as I felt unready for that stage.

Day Seven in the morning we did a silent meditation walk to a river on the other side of the fields. We had to wade across and then laid on the rocks, lounging like lizards, gazing up at the sky. One of the Indian men whom I had partnered with for the cleansing massage earlier in the week and was in my pod, took my hand as we walked. It was just a simple show of affection and was such a wonderful sharing. That evening he left as he was unwell and we didn't even have time to say goodbye. I noticed that this upset me. That unwelcome friend 'rejection' again.

Day Eight morning session was full of dance and afterwards we ended up in the river in our dresses. During sessions we all wore long burgundy smocks, even the men, so that we were all part of the one. In the afternoon the men and women were separated so that we could share separately in the feminine and masculine divine.

Day Nine was our final day and it was dress up time for a carnival. Everyone told me how sweet and pretty I looked. I never saw myself as sweet or particularly pretty and I was just beginning to learn to embrace this truth. I had arranged to go for a walk with Ray in the afternoon but he had left the room when I got back.

So, my expectations of a deepening connection with him didn't materialise. And in actual fact it made it easier for me to let go of any romantic feelings I may have still had left for him. He was not returning to the U.K. with me as he was staying to spend time in India. When I left, he gave me a bar of chocolate and a card. As I sat in the small airport at Dharamshala I opened it. It said 'I love you'.

I was a changed person and little did I know then that this was going to be the start of the best journey of my life.

Chapter 10
The Inevitable

Whilst in India I messaged with Raimon every couple of days. He seemed happy enough to chat and we had some very flirtatious conversations, although of course I was wondering whether he was seeing other women.

I arrived home on the Sunday night and was straight back to work on the Monday. That's conditioned life for you when you only have a certain amount of holiday days a year. I wasn't able to see Raimon until the Thursday evening as Friday was his day off. It felt like an eternity.

I picked him up after his English class as he was staying the night with me. I was so excited to see him and it was reciprocated. It was a beautiful evening and I loved having him in my bed. In the morning we shared a shower together and he drew a heart with R&S in the steam. All seemed wonderful and perfect, and in that moment it was. That day happened to be two months since we had first met and in the sun in the pub garden, we talked about the trip to Scotland at Christmas that he had previously asked me if I would like to go on with him.

I noticed over the weekend that followed my fear of losing Raimon was high and decided that I needed to share how I was feeling with him, ask whether he had seen anyone else and refocus on myself again. I never got the opportunity when I saw him next.

Two days later after a lovely night out at a guitar concert, where Raimon and I had both had a few alcoholic drinks, everything unravelled. I guess we had been on borrowed time. That night there was no love in his heart in our intimacy, it was course rough sex. Not that there is anything wrong with that in a place of love, but I did not feel loved. When he asked if I was OK, thoughtful?! I told him "No", that he showed no care for me. I remember his words so clearly to this day *"I told you I was not so for you"*.

How could he have been so loving and caring up to this point if that was really true. I told him I didn't understand what had happened. He couldn't explain and in that moment I reacted. I couldn't bear to hear another word come from his mouth. I put my clothes on, and left in tears. Alcohol makes me even more emotional than normal. He should have stopped me from leaving, he did try, but obviously not hard enough. I shouldn't have been driving home in that condition, but it was easier for him to just let me go. He didn't even message me to check I had got home safely.

When I wrote this chapter, re-reading the WhatsApp messages we had sent each other, made me feel sad. The emotion it evokes in me is still something I am trying to understand. Rejection can be such an overwhelming consuming emotion and hard to deal with in a rational and objectional way. Perfectly understandable as, after all, it comes from deep routed wounding.

I spent the whole night and following day in tears. Raimon wanted to stay in contact but could I learn to love him unconditionally, as I had now done with Ray, and just be friends. I now know that it was his fear of my love for him, my intensity of staying connected when apart, that scared him so.

I also see now that it was actually me that ended our relationship, because I knew the moment he told me that he was not so for me, before I left for India, that he was an 'unavailable' man.

I learnt to love the reality that Raimon was not available for a romantic relationship. Us breaking up was nothing to do with me, and everything to do with him, and as soon as I could fully accept that, the pain and the tears subsided. Conditioning prevents most people from being able to maintain any kind of relationship after having shared an intimate one. Breaking up and feeling pain is what is expected, right?! Learning to love someone unconditionally is one of the most amazing feelings. You have to take a deep breath and be courageous, but if the person is of such value to you, you will persevere with it, through the heartache and pain to a place of deep connection.

Ten days after the night I ran away we met up and had the most open conversation we had ever had and no sex! I of course was still hoping Raimon wouldn't meet with other women and our sexual relationship lasted for a few more weeks until one evening when he moved too fast on me my instinct just told me to ask him to stop. He did and I told him what was on my mind. I didn't want to have sex with him if he wasn't adoring of me and asked him how he felt about us. He answered me by telling me he had already had sex with two other women. A brave move as he risked losing my friendship. So, his birthday a couple of weeks earlier was to be the last time we had any sexual intimacy. Now every birthday I celebrate with him carries that reminder for me, but maybe that is a good thing to check I am still in the reality of our friendship.

Two weeks later I met with another Tinder date! And a whole new rollercoaster ride was about to begin.

Raimon and I are now the best of friends, who love each other dearly. He can even tell me he loves me. Obviously not in a romantic way. We have taken our relationship to a deeper level, through my unconditional love for him and I guess his for me too, and he is no longer afraid to love me. He is not available to me as a partner and I can now clearly see that he is not 'my man'. The attraction has faded and we now have a very special friendship.

Chapter 11

A man for Christmas - December 2018

Nine days into December I met Joss on tinder and a week later we were meeting up for a walk along the beautiful Sussex canal at Loxwood. Joss is a traveller and he had spent two six-month adventures travelling in a van through Europe so I was keen to know of his experience. Here was someone who could potentially join me on my journey. He had visited all the places I wanted to see and I was feeling a little in awe of his adventure.

I was still trying to adjust to my new relationship with Raimon and meeting another man was the perfect distraction. It feels easier to get over a past love if there is someone new on the scene. But I have come to learn that it actually only suppresses the feelings. As soon as there is a wobble in the relating with the new man the old feelings resurface with a vengeance. I am only ever putting off the inevitable, and in fact drawing out the whole process of letting go and accepting the reality of the situation.

Joss was only a little taller than myself, something that does not normally attract me to a man, but I was in a new state of open mindedness not to let someone's physical form limit me. He was very easy to be with and spoke very mindfully although I sensed a little reservation. We definitely had a connection and I would have loved for him to have taken my hand or kissed me on the river bank. After our walk we ventured into the local pub for a coffee and lingered there for three hours. It seemed neither of us was in a hurry to leave, even though I had a girls Motown night out in Brighton that I had been really looking forward to. I let them know I wasn't going as I just wanted to remain present in the moment. In hindsight, I should have gone out with the girls, as in this moment I was showing Joss an unhealthy dating pattern of focussing my attention all on the man. Although of course in the moment I thought it was just me being present and going with the flow. I have no regrets though as a lovely evening ensued with conversation flowing as Joss and I devoured an exquisitely cooked Moroccan tagine. Morocco is one of the places on my list to travel to in the van. As we sat in his car afterwards, he gave me the most tender kiss. By now it was getting cold so the time had come for me to head home and I did so with a heart full of happiness.

Early the following morning Joss messaged me. It seemed we both had a restless night, thinking about each other and a feeling to be in each other's presence.

We didn't have to wait long as four days later he came over to the house. I was not feeling overly lustful for him, but just being in his presence seemed to fill my soul. We sat on the sofa next to each other for a long time just talking. I'm not sure how long it was before I decided to take the lead and invited him to see my *'altar of love'*. I'm smiling as I write this as we both laughed at my words. The altar of love was actually something I created as a way to honour my inner goddess of love.

Altar of Love with the naked sculpture Ray made and his card

It consists of a large framed picture of a naked goddess with long blue hair caressing her breasts and a bright yellow flower covering her yoni. There are various heart shaped items, candles, fresh wild flowers, peacock feathers and the naked sculpture Ray did of me.

Lovemaking with Joss was slow and intense, full of sexual energy and I got lost looking into the depth of his eyes. In Joss's words "My soul feels rested and content"

The following day he asked me if I had ever seen the Northern Lights. I hadn't, but like so many others, it was on my bucket list. I think it was in that moment I subconsciously decided that I would travel to Norway in the van to see the Aurora Borealis and seven months later that is exactly what I did.

Laksvatnet fjord – Northern lights sighting

Northern Lights - August 30th 2019

Laksvatnet fjord, 50km south of Tromso in Northern Norway. A beautiful spot on a beach by a small lighthouse, surrounded by mountains. The Aurora app said there was a 23% chance at around 10pm. I spoke to a local fisherman on the beach and he said it was too early in the year to be seeing the lights. I was getting cold waiting outside so at 11pm I decided to give up, maybe the fisherman was right. But as I was settling into bed, I took one more look outside the window and there they were. I've never leapt out of bed so fast.

It was a dream come true to see them. They were mostly quite pale green and white but on occasion they were bright green. But this was early in the season so they would only get better over the coming weeks. I sat in the door of the van watching their graceful dance in the night sky for two hours until I was too tired and they were fading. The pictures I took with my iPhone 8 were a disaster but the following month I invested in a Sony camera and a few weeks later I captured some amazing photos.

Abisko National Park - Sweden

I saw Joss again a week later at his mother's cottage, in the Surrey countryside, where he was currently living until he left to travel again. He was keen, *'feeling powerfully compelled towards me'* – his words. I cancelled my planned Christmas trip to North Wales to spend Christmas with Joss as he had asked whether I would like to. The only reason I was going to North Wales was because I didn't want to spend Christmas all alone in my house. North Wales is a place full of wonderful memories for me as I spent time with my father there at a cottage in Snowdonia he owned and later revisited on many trips with friends. It is definitely on my list of places to visit in the van.

I am so glad I chose to spend Christmas with Joss. It was the most perfect time. Hours of massage and making love on a blanket in front of the open fire. The energy flow between us was mind blowing and meditative all at the same time. I had never experienced anything like this before, blissful connection. And in between all of this we walked, talked and played monopoly. I beat Joss every time! which of course I enjoyed as I do have a competitive streak.

Christmas Day was perfect in every way. We started with a two hour walk in the Surrey hills followed by lunch of smoked salmon, couscous, hummus, stuffed peppers, Parma ham and a glass of champagne. Yes, just one. When you are in the high of life you don't need alcohol and Joss isn't a drinker. We even had Christmas crackers, wore the hats and played the cracker charades game. We were both captured by the spirit of Christmas and feeling loved. It certainly will be a Christmas I won't forget in a hurry.

Boxing day, we unsurprisingly had a little less energy but it was still a lovely day of sharing. But when I left the next day, there was an awkwardness between us, we didn't even kiss goodbye, which I only realised as I drove away! Little did I know that the night before was to be the last time we were to share intimacy. My need to stay connected to Joss to alleviate my fear of rejection was more than his capacity for intimacy could hold. We saw each other one more time before he left for his travels.

Every few months I send him a message and I get a polite reply. I'm not sure why I do that because it's not that I am any longer hoping for a relationship with him. In fact, I now see that he is unlikely to be the man I desire in my life, but this doesn't mean he couldn't bring value to my life. But I guess for him it feels a little different.

Chapter 12

Revealing my Plans

In the New Year I told my family of my plans. My children, who were my greatest concern, seemed unphased, but my ex-husband was not at all impressed. He thought I was being entirely selfish and yes, for once maybe I was, if putting your wellbeing first above all else is selfish. But in time he came to terms with my decision and we were able to work amicably through the transition in the best interests of the children. They are all thriving now in their new lives.

As for my friends I don't know anyone who wasn't supportive or even that surprised at my decision. This was so reassuring for me as at times I wondered if I was crazy. It seemed that I would be living a life that a lot of people dreamed of having. But we all have the freedom to follow our dreams by making the choice to step out of our comfort zone.

It doesn't have to be one gigantic leap but just small steps in the direction of your dreams, laying the foundation. Why not start today by asking yourself the question What is my dream? How do I want to live my life?

I promise you it will be the best decision of your life.

Chapter 13

Breakfast on the beach - my Inner Submissive

February arrived along with a breakfast date on the beach from my first Bumble match! Of course, I arrived early, and Alun tested my consciousness of lateness by being late! Did it matter, not at all, especially when I saw him walking towards me, fuck, he was gorgeous, hold it together girl!

I would describe Alun as a pretty mindful person, he meditates and is focussed on self-improvement and is interested in what I have to say. He talks as much as me so I was conscious about trying not to over talk, or zone out. I did both on occasion, but I was fully aware of it. I felt like I could tell this man anything, often the way when I first meet someone. In this moment I seem to have no fear of the outcome, probably because there is no attachment yet. He was very interested in my decision to travel in a campervan, as most people are, and I wanted him to notice that I am an honest, caring and compassionate being. This was later confirmed by his WhatsApp message, "Really loved your company, today, so interesting and very very attentive woman with the softest lips……". Yes, at the end of the two hours, we kissed behind the beach huts, the most wonderful tender long kiss, with passion laying beneath the surface waiting to bubble out.

His WhatsApp message continued; "The next time we meet would you like a healing massage?... Soft candle light flickering heavenly shadows of warmth, soothing deuter music resonating sounds fondling your soul, aromatic warm oil to tease the skin and melt the stresses away from the tired muscles and finally my healing hands to communicate serenity, safety and peace to the unspoken hidden chambers of your being"

My heart somersaulted at the thought. Finally, a man who wants to love and adore me – or so my mind told me.

I tried to be late, stopped off to buy daffodils, as it was St. David's Day, and my sat nav told me I'd arrive at 8.10pm. This would be ten minutes later than the 8pm that Alun had already pushed back to, as he was running behind schedule, of course. He opened the door, fresh from the gym, this 6'4" gorgeous hunk of a man, still behind schedule! I smile, laughing inside. I will always be early and he will always run late. Does it matter, no, but I will try harder next time to be a little later. I have no idea why being late causes me to become anxious - no need to analyse it, just love it the way it is.

As I stepped over the threshold, he kissed me, in the way that you should be kissed, a kiss that becomes a conversation, our lips barely touching to begin with, holding that space between us, feeling each other's breath. Then, slowly he teases my lips with his tongue, sending ripples of pleasure through my entire being. His tongue explores mine, so tenderly but I can feel the passion patiently waiting behind. Then as the passion rises, I step in towards him and moan as I feel his body close to mine, with the energy pulsating between us. In this moment nothing else exists, and I think we could just kiss forever. I pull away; he moans and says "Amazing". Damn, why did I step back? Maybe for fear of the intensity I was feeling in my very soul, as he gently utters words of appreciation. I hand him the daffodils, still clutched in my hand and as he thanks me, he removes a beautiful dead full bloom red rose from a vase replacing it with the daffodils, as I wonder who gave it to him. A likely gift for Valentines, the day he sent me his first message, two weeks ago. A passing thought as this was my moment to be present. There is only really ever this moment. The past has been and the future has not yet happened. At times remembering this has been of great comfort to me, reminding me to be present in each and every day.

We hang out in the kitchen, talking so easily, feeling slightly nervous in anticipation of this amazing massage I have been promised – but it actually never happens! Something else very unexpected did. He offers me wine, although he doesn't drink it himself. It's a fresh crisp white brought by some previous guest. I ask him if he wants to take a shower, as I notice his running late meant that he had not had time before my arrival. As I sit on the sofa waiting for his return, I'm feeling uncomfortable with my knee length leather boots on so I remove them, to just feel into being my most natural self. There is beautiful soft deuter music playing from the television with inspiring images of nature – it's relaxing and I am feeling emotional that I will be in such places when I travel in the van – on my own comes into my mind. I realise as I write we are never on our own, our self is always with us, the one person we can always trust in and who knows us so well.

Alun returns in comfy clothes, a soft fleecy top – he is being himself. I ask him about his upcoming trip to Los Angeles to attend a Tony Robbins event 'Unleash the Power Within'. Tony Robbins is an American motivational speaker and philanthropist. I'm feeling sad he is going; my attachment is already noticeable even though this is only our second date!

Conversation is a bit of a blur; he mentions something about a 'gut buster' breakfast which instantly brings back memories of late-night breakfasts after a night of dancing and drinking at the 'Ocean rooms' in Brighton. But for some reason I call them the 'red rooms', shit, where is my mind at! We smile at each other in that naughty knowing way, his smile penetrating my every fibre, and my mind is running amok with thoughts of the book *'Fifty Shades of Grey'*. My voice passively follows the lead mentioning that my friends love the idea of being dominated and the 'red room of pain' but would likely never actually experience it. What am I saying? I know it's been a while since I've had sex but seriously?! Alun says he has some toys and would I like to see them. I'm intrigued and how can I back down now, so I nod. I see now that this was the defining moment of everything that was to follow over the next weeks. Later in our relating, I wish I had said 'No' in this moment and told him how much I had been looking forward to the sensual healing massage. This story may have taken a completely different path. But I didn't.

What was to follow was a very different kind of healing to what I had been expecting that evening. I say healing because if we allow ourselves to be uninhibited and unashamed in our sexual desires it can be a very healing and liberating process, as it was for me that evening. The pleasure reached a level I had never experienced before. An extract from the book 'The Awakened Woman' by Tererai Trent. "Awakened to our own desires, our own erotic vitality these self-connections make us feel alive and from that place of aliveness with the erotic self, then it's much easier for us to connect to our work, our relationships and our dreams".

Alun returns a few moments later with cuffs on a chain, a paddle and a neck collar with nipple clamps that I did not notice at first. I vaguely remember him asking me if I was OK with this as he put the cuffs on me and asks me about the tattoo on my wrist. I could hardly get the words out about Haiti and my spiritual experience there as I was too distracted by him fixing the collar around my neck and then blindfolding me. I loved the feeling of powerlessness although of course I was totally in control of everything that followed. I mean I could have told him to stop, and I felt safe in the belief that he would have done so. He lay me on the sofa and kissed me, whispering what he was going to do, the most beautiful pleasurable things. My body was on fire. As he kissed every part of me, whispering, I was completely lost in the sensations spiralling through my body. My brain being triggered to fire all those sensors under the skins surface and I could feel the energy in my body rising and I knew I was going to be so very wet, my juices flowing with abandon, just as I was feeling.

After an indefinable period of time Alun asked me to change position to expose another part of my body to him and of course I obeyed without question. Why would I not? I wanted more. "Kneel on the sofa with your arse in the air". I felt his tongue on my clit, my ass, transitioning from soft gentle movement to flicking and sucking. I was at the edge of orgasm and each time I felt I was tipping over the precipice I told him intuitively as I knew he wouldn't want me to reach orgasm just yet. And I didn't want to, I didn't want this heightened pleasurable experience to end.

Alun called me a 'good girl', a major trigger for me, and would stop what he was doing only to move me into yet another compromising position to bring me again to the peak of almost oblivion.

He told me to lay over his lap, and of course I knew what was coming next. I felt the first spank, hard enough to send pain triggers but gentle enough not to really hurt. He tells me he is not into giving pain – only pleasure. Every now and again I felt the intensity of the nipple clamps.

Sometime later he leads me to the bedroom. I am excitedly anticipating him removing his clothes so that I can finally feel his skin beneath my touch. But first he gently pushes me against the wall and asks me to stick my arse out. This is when he uses the dildo, it's all just too much so he picks me up effortlessly and lays me on his bed, and takes off his clothes. He returns to pussy licking, telling me how beautiful I taste and what an amazing body I have. His words make me feel incredibly desirable. Then I feel his cock on my mouth, and as I explore it, I nearly freak out, it was so freaking thick I could barely get my mouth around it. Not something I have encountered before so I feel a little fear but as I hear his moaning it encourages me to show him how much I love pleasuring cock. I run my lips and tongue down the side of his thick sheath, just wanting to bring pleasure. I kiss and suck gently on his scrotum and everywhere I can reach.

After a while he lays on top of me and hands me the vibrator. He knows he needs to go slow and gradually I open up for him. The fear is keeping me tight and his penetration hurts a little but he knows every way to help me flower for him. We move slowly from one position to another discovering what feels most enjoyable. I grab the vibrator and he is able to penetrate further and I tell him he can fuck me whenever he wants. He duly obeys and I look at his face in ecstasy as I ride waves of orgasm. At some point I had removed the blindfold desiring to see and take in everything that I was feeling. I continued to suck and massage his cock until he could bear it no longer and asked if I wanted him to come. I caressed his balls with my tongue and mouth and ran my fingers down the inside of his thighs and then my tongue in all those sensitive places. He loved it and came and I gently sucked his cock and tasted his come.

I love the relaxed and content feeling that comes after satiation and I am never in a hurry to leave that moment. Just bathing in the intimacy shared. At some point he gave me his dressing gown and made me a cup of tea and we sat on the sofa and talked and kissed and drank tea. He told me I was so really really beautiful and have the most amazing smile that lights up my face. I told him I found it difficult to believe I was that beautiful and he seemed to understand what I was saying. Today I look in the mirror and I happy to say I see that beauty. Not because I think I have the most stunning of looks but because the beauty of who I am inside radiates out.

I didn't stay that night as he was getting up early the following morning. I didn't ask why but on the drive home I notice that I wished he would have desired me to stay. I was feeling that fear of rejection, despite everything that he had said to me. Even now rejection is my biggest fear, despite knowing that I will always get through it, if it happens. When I feel rejection, I feel such pain which is sometimes unbearable and I wish I didn't experience this but I know that I just need to ride that wave. I don't know if I will ever conquer this fear, it is so deep routed in my childhood, but I know all I can do is love myself just as I am. Love that I notice this pain is there to heal me knowing that it is an opportunity to love myself more and to grow in awareness. Just like the pain the body gives us when there is something wrong with us, the mind does the same, inviting us to dive deeper into what lies beneath.

In that moment I put on Barry Manilow, I know so cheesy, and "Can't take my eyes of you" started playing. A song that I danced to so much when I was a teenager. From there on in this has been my song for Alun. Every time I hear it, I have such a smile on my face. Although there was a moment that the so-called rejection came from him that I was sobbing to it. It is all good now though and I as I write this I am smiling. Maybe he will too when he reads this.

Chapter 14

Waiting for Love - or Lust?

"I love your energy, your taste coating my chin in erotic euphoric frenzied tongue-lashing sweet juices of yours. Love your beautiful face and your sylph like figure in my bed making you my woman, my good girl. Slave to wanton passions unrestrainedly"
– Alun

A week later Alun left for ten days to Los Angeles. I had of course wanted to see him before he went but this sadly did not happen. However, he was very attentive with sending regular messages whilst he was away. One asking me if I had ever experienced intimacy with a woman before or had any ambition to? What the fuck? Now that was unexpected – or was it?!

His first voice message to me when he got back. "I'd love to get together and just completely rock your world to be honest. Hopefully you will allow me to carry on from where we left off? I'd like to blindfold you, tie your wrists together and have me and a lady friend of mine spoil you. What I mean by that is touch your skin, very lightly, tease you, tease your mouth, your tongue, your face, your neck, your shoulders, your arms, your fingers, your breasts, your nipples, especially your nipples, your belly, your belly button, the inside of your thighs, the back of your knees, your ankles, the outside of your thighs and then feeling two tongues on your pussy. One of us would be pulling one side of your swollen lips and the other person would be sucking and licking the other side of your swollen lips. I want you to feel the sensation of a tongue on the very swollen part of your clit, feather flicking actions from the top of the tongue and feather flicking actions of the other person's tongue on your ass. Licking your ass, probing your ass so it's going inside of your ass as well as sucking on your clit. So, you have two people intensely working on you. I want you to feel your pussy pulsing as you can imagine that happening. And I will leave the woman to devour your pussy drinking all your juices. I want you to feel the tongue fucking your pussy as it goes in and out, feeling the woman's nose buried into your clit. I want you to feel your juices being completely manipulated. And whilst she's doing that, I'll be softly kissing your lips, our tongues enmeshed, kissing sensually. I'll be stroking your face very gently as my hand travels down your neck on to your breasts, just manipulating and squeezing your breasts. I want you to feel the connection, I want you to feel my breath upon yours. I want you to feel the softness and sensual feeling and energy coming from me. I want you to feel just how good I feel when I'm kissing you, when I'm near you. And all the while you've got this woman's tongue licking your pussy and she's taking you to places that would not be particularly described well without expressing the deep vulnerable powerful explosiveness that shudders through the soul as you're commanded by the pleasure-seeking energy of an inquisitive tongue. Lashing between your swollen lips as your juices splutter uncontrollably devoured and the lovely mix and contrast of my sensuous kissing. And when your juices are spluttering your thighs are squeezed together, I will then stroke you some more allowing your breath and body to recover and pushing you on to your front allowing us both to kiss your back, the back of your legs, whispering into your ear my intention. And then swapping places as I kiss the back of your leg and seeing her run her tongue up your spine, the back of your neck and she'll be biting at your ear telling you what she's going to do next, with her strap on"

"I thought I would just give you a mental picture, an idea to see what of that you might like or not like. I'd be very interested in your thoughts. As you can tell I'm super horny right now, please forgive me but the fact that you are going to hear this message and knowing that it can be a reality is extremely powerful. Anyway, have a lovely evening and hope to hear from you soon".

I only saw Alun twice more. It seemed he had another life, which I was not completely oblivious to. Although he had never mentioned another woman, I had sensed it and had noticed that his location on Bumble had been one particular place (not his home) on a regular basis. I was still hoping to see him one more time right up until the day I left in the van, but it never materialised.

Chapter 15

'Meet Lucy'

On March 5th 2019 I picked up the van. It was a beautiful sunny Spring day and I was so excited. I was still working until the end of March and then I had one month to pack up everything in the house ready for its one-year rental.

I had nicknamed the van 'The Love Van', for that which I was searching, real love of myself. For without that how can you truly be the best version of yourself out in the world. But I also decided that she was deserved of a proper name and so she was called 'Lucy'. Really just because I felt it went well with the word Love; Lucy Love.

Before I even had the van, whilst browsing in a craft shop, I had found some beautiful letters carved into heart shapes in balsam wood that could be strung up. And, of course, I bought the letters that made up the word love as the perfect décor for the van.

The van is very eco-friendly and energy efficient. There is a rechargeable lithium battery to power everything inside the van from the lights to the fridge which can be recharged from the solar panel on the roof. The gas stove uses LPG and the van has an eco-driving mode and an AdBlue system which reduces harmful emissions.

Before my solo maiden voyage, I took a mini break with a dear friend to the much-loved country retreat of Her Majesty the Queen - Sandringham Estate in Norfolk. A place that we had both wanted to visit but never had. We stayed at the camp site on the estate, a very posh initiation to van life. It was a great way to see how it felt driving a couple of hundred miles and sleeping in the van. I loved it.

Sandringham Estate - Norfolk

Chapter 16
Van Life Begins - April 2019

My first destination in the van just had to be Gretna Green. Not just because it's the first place over the border in Scotland but because it is one of the most infamous historic places of love in the U.K. For those who don't know the history of Gretna Green.

In the middle of the 18th-century English lords approved new laws to tighten marriage arrangements. Couples had to reach the age of twenty-one before they could marry without their parents' consent and their marriage had to take place in a church. Scottish law, however, was different: You could marry on the spot, in a simple 'marriage by declaration', or 'handfasting' ceremony, only requiring two witnesses and assurances from the couple that they were both free to marry. With such a relaxed arrangement within reach of England, it soon led to the inevitable influx of countless thousands of young couples running-away to marry over the border and Gretna Green was the first village they would have arrived at.

I have a vague memory when I was sixteen years of age and dating an older man of twenty-five (crazy I know), that this romantic pilgrimage could be for me. Thank goodness it never happened, but I still like the idea of getting married in the simple surroundings of what used to be the Blacksmiths. Even today, to seal the marriage the anvil is struck with the blacksmiths hammer.

So, as part of my quest on this journey of love of myself, others and the world how could I not make this my first port of call. As I arrived a couple had recently wed and were standing outside the old blacksmiths and I somehow managed to take a quick photo whilst driving towards it.

The Old Blacksmiths

I parked Lucy in front of the word 'LOVE' created from different colour locks on a metal frame. Locks with the names of couples in love. Gretna Green is a very small village and although behind the blacksmiths there are a few touristy shops it hasn't been spoilt, although I can imagine in the high season the number of tourists here would completely take away from the feel of the place.

There is a fun love maze with the reward being a beautiful view of the surrounding countryside and being able to touch what is supposedly the original anvil of the blacksmiths. Touching it is supposed to bring good fortune in affairs of the heart. Well in hind sight, a year later, I can say it certainly brought a few men into my heart.

That evening it took me an hour to find a spot with a nice view that I felt comfortable with to park up for the night around the lanes of Gretna Green. Being my first night of wild camping I was a little uncertain, especially as I was parked next to gates of a field and thought the farmer may pitch up at any point. All was well, and it turned out to be the perfect spot. I threw a very quick dinner together of cold quiche, baked beans and salad, as by this point, I was starving.

It wasn't long after that I decided to get the van ready for the night, as after the driving and excitement of arriving in Scotland I was pretty tired. When the bed is out, it's so cosy and for a while I read a book that I had been given by a friend *'How to Live in a van and travel'* written by Mike Hudson, aka "Vandogtraveller", a young man in his twenties who has done exactly as I have back in 2015 and is still travelling! What a great dream to accomplish at such a young age, although I think the older you get the more stuck in conditioning you can become and the harder it is to break free. When I finally turned out the lights, with the blackout curtains pulled, it was pitch black, as there is no light pollution on a country lane in Scotland. I couldn't even see my hand in front of me! It felt quite strange but I soon settled into it and was asleep in no time at all. Although I woke a couple of times in the night, I soon fell back to sleep and ended up having a good eight hours. I actually sleep far better in the van now than I do in a bed in a house.

In the morning it turns out that it takes a good hour to get the van ready to travel again and add on to this getting washed and dressed, having breakfast, that's two hours! But when time no longer matters as you don't have to get to work or drop children off at school, how long something takes is irrelevant. You have to learn to let go of the feeling of having to do anything by a certain time, and just go with the flow of life.

I'm not going to document my entire van life journey in this book, as I have already done that in my blogs and on my YouTube channel mindfulvanlife but I will certainly be mentioning those places that have been significant and inspirational for me both emotionally and mindfully.

The following day after producing my first blog I headed to Pollok Country Park which is three miles outside of Glasgow. The drive to Scotland was a little scary up and over the mountains, as I have a fear of feeling high up and of heights. Something that I knew that I would have to push through when travelling in the van and it was nothing to what I would encounter in Norway. I stealth camped at the country park, behind the woods of one of the carparks as I was uncertain whether you were allowed to stay overnight. There were no signs saying you couldn't and there were a few other campervans in the carpark which reassured me. It is a beautiful park with a lovely country house to explore and a river meandering through acres of grounds. The best part is it's entirely free, you don't even have to pay to park and it's just a five-minute walk to the train station to get the train directly into Glasgow.

Stealth camping with the roof down

I had been feeling a little stress at times over the last couple of days but I think that was just fear related and I knew once I settled into my new way of life it would be fine. There were and have continued to be moments of laughter of disbelief that I feel truly free. However, there has always been a sense of guilt about leaving my children. Less so now, as I see them flourish in their lives without me constantly mothering them, but it goes against all my motherly instincts and love not to be with them. But I know that I am setting them an example that you can live the life you choose without fear or judgement and don't have to follow the conditioning of life. I have had waves of emotion of loneliness, recognising that you can be in the most amazing place but feel incredibly alone, and just wishing you had someone by your side to share it all with.

The van really felt like home in such a short space of time and I became very organised very quickly. Everything has its place (no more leaving things on the side) and I soon established a morning and night routine. This way I have everything I need, where I need it, at the time I need it. Like the porta potty and toilet roll in the middle of the night, or the kettle ready filled on the stove for a cup of tea first thing in the morning in bed! I don't even have to go downstairs to make it. Bliss, unless of course I forget to put the cup out with the teabag in. What a problem to have!

One week in and I have learnt so much already. I have learnt that I do not need to worry so much about where I can empty the porta potty or where I can get water. When you trust in the flow of life it provides what you need exactly when you need it. It's an amazing realisation. In conditioned life we're always trying to plan and control everything, so we feel safe and know where we are headed. But when we let go of that, that's when you truly live in the flow of life, not constantly battling against it. In just a week life has provided water when I needed it, and even a kettle to boil water at an honesty shop when I was on a tiny beach in Mull and my gas stopped working.

I'm thinking of all the times something like this happened to me in the last year and it's truly incredible. I think it's possible you can only understand this sense of being provided for when you experience it. One time I got stuck on a track in the middle of nowhere in the Sierra Navada mountains in Southern Spain and just as I was wondering what I needed to do some Spanish workers arrived and helped me.

I've loved every moment of my first week of travel. It seems longer and choosing Scotland to get acquainted with van life was definitely the right decision. Venturing out alone but not too far from home, so still a degree of feeling safe.

Loch Lomond

Van life Day 10

Today I drove to Carsaig (on the island of Mull) so I could walk to Carsaig Arches, sea caves created by sea erosion, a three-mile trek on a coastal path. Whenever I go out, I always ensure I wear my bikini, even when the temperature is only ten degrees, just in case I get an opportunity to wash in a river or shower in a waterfall. There is something uniquely invigorating about cleansing yourself in nature. Today did not disappoint as I found several waterfalls, although the water was absolutely freezing but I felt so warm once I got out despite the cold.

Carsaig Arches

When your mind becomes empty of everyday stresses and tasks it creates space. Whilst walking along this tricky coastal path, it came to my mind that life was a journey just like this. As we navigate through life it is very rarely just easy going. Like the path I was on, full of rocks and waterways, that I needed to navigate. There is no point feeling upset or frustrated about this as this is how the path has been crafted by nature, as our life's path is there as it is. All we can do is manoeuvre through it as best we can. Sometimes it will become bumpy and we just have to keep going knowing that we can overcome this period. Sometimes we lose our way and we just need to let our gut feeling/instinct carry us through until we find the path again. Often, we are unsure of what/where our true path lies or *'who we really are'*. There is no hurry to find that, just be patient and it will show itself again. Sometimes we will lose our way completely and then we must trust and be open to life to set us back on our way again. Other times there maybe two paths we could take and we have to make a choice but there is no right or wrong path. We must be brave enough to choose otherwise we will become stuck.

All of this from a walk.

Chapter 17

A Birthday Alone - May 2019

My first birthday ever on my own, waking up in the van on the beautiful beach of Uisken on the island of Mull. The day started off with me having a bit of a cry, feeling sorry for myself being all on my own, still without a man in my life to adore and cherish me and spoil me on this day. Sometimes I do wonder if this is what life has in store for me. But then I remember that my man is out there in the world waiting for us to meet. He will only arrive when it is the right time for both of us. I just hope it's not too long! I would at least like to enjoy some of my life with him whilst I am still active and healthy.

I actually ended up having a great day. I visited the beautiful island of Iona, reputed to be the resting place of sixty kings. Only the islanders are allowed to take cars to the island so I took my bike which meant that I could explore the whole length of Iona (only 3 miles) in a couple of hours. As soon as you arrive there you have the feeling of being on the Mediterranean coast line. The sea is that bluey green colour and so crystal clear, under the beautiful sunshine of the day. At the northern end of the island, past the Cathedral, there are several large beautiful deserted white sand beaches – maybe not quite so deserted in the summer months.

I did not go into the Cathedral as you had to pay £7.10 (not expensive really but outside of my budget). I was already treating myself to tea and cake later on at one of the hotels, nothing posh mind you! I really have learnt to be strict with my budget, otherwise the simple truth is that I will run out of money. This has also really brought me a real appreciation of when I do treat myself. Later whilst eating my cake, I met a really lovely lady, called Helen, and we had an in-depth conversation about travelling and life in general and headed back on the ferry together. She is now following my blog, thank you Helen for sharing my special day.

I ended the day getting drunk on the bottle of champagne that Sussex Campervans had given me when I collected the van. Champagne is my favourite tipple, albeit an expensive one, so unlikely to happen again anytime soon – outside the budget!

Uisken Beach - Mull

Then in my hour of loneliness and a desire to feel loved I set to browsing the dating apps and met Ross, a twenty-nine-year-old living in Glasgow. No judgement please, that is just conditioning, we are two consenting adults. Two days later we had set up a date to meet in Edinburgh in two weeks' time. I even invited him to stay over in the van in the Pentland Hills, just outside Edinburgh; if we got on of course. It felt a bit crazy, but once again I was needing a little loving and he came across as a really nice guy. It's not so much about having sex for me, but sharing intimacy and of course the sex is always very pleasurable.

We would of course initially meet in a public place – just in case he was using a fake profile. But I am guided by my intuition when I meet men from the dating apps. And ok they may not have been 'my man' but they have all been good guys.

Chapter 18

Letting Go

After sending this picture to Alun of me sunbathing in my bikini on the shores of the Loch at Glencoe, Scotland, in twenty-one degrees of heat in mid-May, I receive a voicemail from him.

His message said "I've used sex to numb my pain from my younger years and as a consequence I've had a very interesting time since coming out of my marriage. But for me to get to a better place I have to cut out my usual method of numbing, distracting and diluting pain from the past. So, this message is to explain that as much as I find you extremely extremely attractive and I know there is a lovely connection there too, I'm going to have to take a break from any physical contact and any temptation, in order to go through this period when I can face and sit with the inner feelings that I have been basically freezing. I'll keep your number if that is ok and contact you in a distant time where I can hopefully reconnect and see where you are in your life. Could be six months, could be a year, I'm not sure. All I know is that I've got to do this for me and as hard as it is, I have to communicate this with you so you know I haven't just fallen off the planet. I have real intention for being healthier on an emotional level. I wish you all the best, I really do. You take care".

I had been expecting to meet up with Alun on my return to England in June but there it was, the time for me to start the letting go process all over again, which began with tears flowing down my cheeks at the side of the loch in the beautiful Scottish Spring sunshine. It was the perfect place to start the healing process.

When I feel rejected my feelings of not being loved overwhelm me. I have always been subconsciously attracted to men that will ultimately bring me this pain. I've learnt recently that the excitement and attraction I feel comes from eroticizing rejection. It feeds that part of me that still feels like I need to prove that I am worthy of being loved. This is just familiar unhealthy dating patterns playing out. I am happy to say that this is now something I am fully aware of and am now trying to date only emotionally available men who are truly available for a relationship and who will cherish and honour me and treat the relationship as sacred. Who knows, by the time this book is published I may have found 'my man'.

River Foyers - Inverness

Chapter 19

Toy Boy in Edinburgh

We met outside Edinburgh station on a damp Scottish Saturday. His train was running late so I was a little cold by the time he pitched up. He looked nice and had a lovely sounding voice, with a gentle Scottish lilt to it, and very polite. I was simply relieved that he was the person from the photos because you never know until you meet someone if they are using photos of themselves. Of course, you can always have a video call or check them out on other social media sites before you meet. I didn't completely fancy him straight off, but I have learnt to always keep an open mind as attraction is not just based on one's appearance. We walked up Carlton Hill for a view of the city but the weather was really not very conducive for sightseeing as it had started to rain so we decided to find a pub to wait out the weather. After a couple of large gin and tonics, some food and nice conversation I was feeling relaxed and open to Ross spending the night with me. After checking in with him that this was what he still wanted to do, we headed to the Royal mile and the Castle for a quick selfie and then the Scottish museum, as it is free. But time had run away from us and it was closing. We bought some food and alcohol for dinner and set off back to the van at the park and ride. Originally, I was going to stay the night there but it all felt a little seedy so we decided it would be nicer to drive to the Pentland Hills, which was only half an hour away.

We found a lovely little wooded carpark at Flotterstone, right where the trails into the Pentland Hills begin. It even had a café and a toilet block. Pure luxury. Ross had a beer and I had a glass of wine and we sat and chatted for quite some time until I felt the urge to ask him to kiss me. It wasn't long before we got the bed out! It was all very loving and gentle. He had a great arse and very strong manly thighs from all the hiking he does. In this moment he was more of a receiver than a giver but it was still enjoyable and he loved what I had to offer and it didn't take long to get him really horny. We made love twice that evening and again in the morning, after I showed him the lovers sitting position that I had learnt at the tantra retreat in India. With the man sitting the woman straddles him and wraps her legs around him which allows a very intimate hug. I was quite nicely surprised at his aptitude and longevity for someone so young.

After a hearty breakfast of scrambled egg on toast, as we had skipped dinner, we went out for a short hike in the hills. It was all very pleasant although Ross wasn't very tactile; he didn't take my hand or hug or kiss me at all whilst we were out walking.

Afterwards, we sat and had a coffee at the café before I dropped him back at the train station and then went exploring to another part of the Pentland Hills.

The following evening, I returned to Flotterstone and I was feeling emotional about being there without Ross and was missing his company. I was interested to see how I would feel after casual sex, where there was almost certainty of no future outcome of any kind. Because this was likely going to be the only kind of relationship that I was going to be able to have whilst travelling. I felt aloneness, just wanting to have someone else around. I was still striving to be happy with just being with myself so much of the time. I knew now I needed to just let go of him. But for me this is easier said than done because I form attachment very quickly.

We continued to message and three weeks later I booked a last-minute flight, with my British Airways avios points, and flew to Glasgow from Gatwick (as I was then back in Sussex) to spend four days with him. It was great seeing the route I had driven in the van from the air. However, not really the best way to let go!

I flew Club class as that's the seat that was available with the points. To me, after being in the van, it was the pinnacle of luxury, being waited on with an unlimited supply of alcohol and real cutlery. Van life had already certainly given me a real appreciation for pleasures such as this. It was a great start to my 'dirty' weekend away. As I write this, I realise I really don't like this term. There is absolutely nothing dirty about allowing yourself to spend pleasurable loving time with another person. I see it as a mutual act of affection and love, I'm smiling.

Ross was a gentleman from the moment he picked me up at the airport. It was great to see him, although once we got back to his flat, I could sense he was feeling a little awkward so I asked if he would like a massage. We ended up spending the entire afternoon in bed. A great way to break the ice. He was learning that it was very pleasurable to go slow and not rush for an outcome of orgasm, and of course with that came more pleasurable receiving for me too. I think his lack of attentiveness when we first met was more a lack of confidence and him being out of his comfort zone being with an older woman and more experienced lover. He was the youngest man I've been intimate with and I am his oldest woman by far, not that age is important. It's more about emotional maturity and connection.

It does seem that there are a lot of men in their thirties who have an older woman on their bucket list!

The following day we went for a lovely walk in the hills and that evening Ross cooked a delicious stir fry. I get such delight from watching a man cook, such a simple thing that makes me feel looked after. He's so adorable.

On the Monday Ross went to work and I played house! I did a bit of cleaning, went to the shop and had a walk. It felt amusing when he sent me a text message telling me when he'd be home and when he walked in the door, I had dinner on the go. It must have been a little strange for him too, to have a woman in his home.

Our final night together did not disappoint. It was a culmination of everything we had learnt brought each other pleasure. He gave me a lovely sensual and sexual massage and I loved witnessing how comfortable and confident he had become with me. It was the perfect end to a beautiful weekend and the last time I was to see him.

Our relating gradually faded over time but every now and again I will send him a text message to see how he is and he always replies. Just a genuinely nice guy.

Chapter 20

A Reality Check - June 2019

I returned to Sussex for a very special friend's wedding on Cooden beach in Bexhill. A couple I have known for twenty years! and part of the amdram theatre group that I had been a member of for even longer. There were so many friends there to catch up with. It was a very romantic affair, especially as they had been together for fifteen years. An inspiring example of real love and a truly beautiful day blessed with friendship and sunshine.

The next couple of weeks were unashamedly spent catching up with more friends, being pampered and feeling a little guilty about taking time out from van life. After all, I had only been living in the van for five weeks and had only really just settled into it. It had been very emotional for me when the time came to leave Scotland and head back down south. My biggest fear was being pulled back in to the conditioning of everyone else's lives. I realised when I saw the children again this was going to be inevitable especially as I would be staying at the family house with them for two weeks before leaving again as their Dad, was going on holiday with his new partner.

Those last two weeks were challenging, although I had still been sleeping in the van on the driveway to help keep me grounded. I was starting to feel fearful all over again about leaving, saying goodbye once again to the children and facing an even bigger challenge of driving through Europe to Norway. But that really was going to be an adventure of a life time.

Chapter 21

Europe beckons

I left the UK July 14th 2019 via the Eurotunnel paid for with Tesco supermarket vouchers. Every little helps, and it truly is appreciated when you no longer have an income.

My first stop was to be Dunkirk. It seemed fitting to pay my respects to those who had given their lives for the freedom I now have. It was very poignant and humbling seeing the solid lines of the white headstones of the soldiers that had died here and then standing on the very beach that so many had been rescued from during the evacuation in World War II.

From here I headed to Lockeren Nature Reserve in Belgium where I spent a delightful night watching the partial eclipse of the full moon. The next day I was to head to the city of Antwerp. I don't really enjoy driving into cities but here you can park on the outskirts and use the Park and Ride. It is a very picturesque historic city with beautiful buildings abound and cobbled streets. It is also the centre of the world diamond trade, another showing of love on my journey. No other gemstone conveys human emotion more powerfully than a diamond. These stones are magical, earth-grown, rare and timeless and it is these qualities that have made them the perfect symbol of eternal love, commitment, and romance.

Antwerp City Hall with flags of all nations

From a city of love, I travelled to the city of International Peace and Justice, The Hague. Of course, being such a famous city, I felt I should take a look and I'm so glad I did. I was a bit concerned about where I was going to park the van for an overnight stay but I know now that I never need worry as life always seems to find a way of giving me the perfect spot. As I drove in, I came across the beautiful Westbroekpark where I found free parking (I think the only free parking in the city) and just a cycle ride away from the centre on their amazing cycle paths.

The Peace Palace

I wasn't looking forward to the next part of my journey as it was to take me over the Afsluitdijk dyke. A dyke road of 32km that connects Noord-Holand and Friesland. My fear was that it would be high and there is water on both sides, but as is often the case my fear was unfounded. It's not that high and it is pretty wide but it is a very weird feeling driving across it, knowing that it is holding back the sea and being surrounded by water.

Parked on the De Nieuwe Afsluitdijk feeling like a boat!

Onward to Emmerdennen. I always choose places to stay that are in or very near to nature and in this particular place there are Hunebedden (megalithic tombs) the oldest monuments in the Netherlands. They are pretty impressive and over 5000 years old.

Hunebedden

Onward to Germany and a slight diversion to the peninsular of Nordstrand on the North Sea coast as it looked like an interesting spot in nature. I drove right to the very end as I had learnt from my time in Scotland, this is how you find the very best places and it didn't disappoint. The marshes on one side and the North Sea on the other.

A new day and I arrived in my next country - Denmark at Skjern Enge in a nature reserve of 2200 hectares consisting mainly of meadows, wetlands and lakes. It's located in Denmark's only delta and is a pretty impressive place. It took almost twenty years to complete Northern Europe's largest nature restoration project, and the result is unparalleled. Skjern Enge has once again become one of Northern Europe's most important rest areas for wading and water birds. It was here that I met this amazing family from Ireland who were living in their van, forging an alternative life for themselves and their three children, a baby on the way and a new puppy! They had my complete respect.

Onward to Klitmoller Strand in Thisted. This is a huge expanse of golden sand beach. It was here that I took my author selfie. It is just the beginnings of the beautiful and wild Thy National park which is the last wilderness left in Denmark. It is an area of long coastlines, the most enormous sand dunes I have ever seen, heaths, lakes and forests with the tallest pine trees and wonderful sunsets.

It came to my attention, that I would never have experienced any of these amazing places in nature, if I hadn't of been travelling in the van. It is truly an awe inspiring and unique experience.

Klimoller Strand Thistead

And finally, the day had come that I was to board the ferry from Hirtshalls to Kristiansand in Norway.

Chapter 22

Love and trust in the flow of life

I wasn't going to use the dating apps again, as I had decided to trust life to bring a man into my life at the right moment. But I had just arrived in Norway and had drunk champagne (again), the sun was shining and I was parked in a beautiful location at the foot of mountains on Lyngdal fjord. I was in love with this magical place already.

The only thing missing was someone to share the moment with, a repeating theme I know. I had swiped left on the few men on Bumble in the area and had resorted to Tinder. There he was, Adam, thirty-two years of age, with a picture of a kitten and a profile just as cute. And we matched! But he was in London because Tinder hadn't reset my location.

However, it turned out he is as much a dreamer as I am. Only a few days into our relating Adam mentioned about coming to Norway to meet me and beyond that coming to visit me often, three to five days every few weeks. He seemed very mindful and conscious of living a healthy life, loved what I was doing, and said I was living his dream. He called me inspiring and felt I could be his soul mate. We felt we were perfect for each other. How foolish we were in that moment when we hadn't even met. But we both wanted to open our hearts to each other and in that moment that was all that mattered.

Aside from this he was an entrepreneur, made his money early in life from social media and I was soon to learn that he could help me with expanding my audience. How more perfect, in this moment, could this man have been for me. Someone to share some of my journey with, be intimate with and help me inspire others.

We messaged every day, some very long conversations, for the four and a half weeks leading up to his arrival in Norway, and a few phone conversations too. Every day I would share photos of the amazing mountains and fiords along my journey. It felt good apart from the…..

Flekkefjord – Magma Geopark

Naeroyfjord

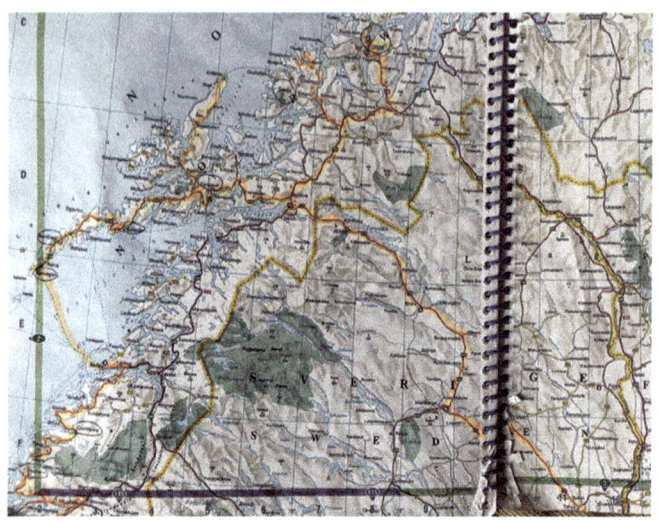

My route up the North-west coast of Norway and down through
Sweden highlighted in orange

Chapter 23

Rejection

"I'm available-ish now, I think later I maybe going…..!" Just in that one moment as I read those words I began to cry. Yet another guy who is not showing up for me. He had said we could absolutely have a phone call today and now?… Well now I know that we won't. That is the reality. Why do I feel such a sense of rejection? Because I know he's not showing up for me. This is the point I will start making excuses, find good reasons why we're not having the phone call, why he's only available-ish for me. Reasons that will allow me to continue this 'relating' that has barely begun. Just a week ago he was so keen to speak with me on the phone, and we had had the most wonderful two-hour phone conversation on a Sunday morning. And now?…

I'm sensing the red flag yet I know that I am still going to give him another chance. He won't even realise what has happened. If I mention it, he may well think I am overreacting and maybe I am. One of the downfalls of having so much available time on your own is that you look forward to connecting with someone you can have a real conversation with.

When we do actually talk, I am going to ask him to show up for me by suggesting he actually books the flight to Norway to meet me. After all he was supposed to be with me last weekend but he left booking the flight to the last minute and then there was no availability. However, it worked out for the best for him as he wouldn't have been able to take the flight due to a friend's death. See how good I am at finding very valid reasons.

I've also got a hero job for him, to bring out a LPG gas converter as the one I was given is not right and I am soon going to be out of gas. Fortunately, I am not totally reliant on him as if he doesn't come, I can get it myself when I fly back in September for my daughter's eighteenth birthday. But I am giving him every opportunity to demonstrate he can show up for me. If he doesn't, then I know I should be cutting him loose, despite the fact that he can help me with my digital media campaign on Instagram to market this book I am sitting here writing.

When we did finally talk, three days later, I explained about how he could be my hero which would mean him booking the flight. Despite a lovely chat, I sensed something – couldn't quite put my finger on it at the time but a day later he confessed to being separated and having two young girls. How on earth could he have kept this from me in four weeks of conversation. I had mentioned my separation and children on several occasions and not once did he say anything. He said he wanted to tell me when we met so we could discuss it. It turns out he is not able to be as free as he might like to be. What hurts the most is the deceit, when I thought we were only with the truth. I think he may be right when he says his family think that he is living in a dream. I don't doubt that he wants to meet, just that he will never actually be able to. So at least I know now, and it is my choice whether to continue with this 'dream'.

Today I crossed into the Arctic Circle on a ferry crossing from Kilboghamn to Jektvik on the northwest coast of Norway. It was an incredible feeling knowing that I had made it this far and I was still heading further North to the Lofoten Islands.

Chapter 24

A Van Life Day

I normally wake naturally around 7am and depending on the weather or if I am driving that day determines how long I linger in bed. My first task is always to make myself a cup of tea from my bed. The stove is conveniently close and as I drink my tea, I will wonder on the day ahead.

Glomfjord next to a waterfall

After tea it's time for my skin care ritual. Since travelling in the van and being in natures elements every day, I made the decision to finally really take care of my skin in the way it deserves. I've never really spent a lot of money on skin care products in the past but as part of loving myself more it was time. I chose to invest in a natural, organic skincare product that complements my new lifestyle and I am sure I am looking younger now than when I first started this journey!

I then get dressed, put the bed away and have some breakfast. If I am driving that day, I will get everything ready in the van for leaving. By this time normally two hours has flown by.

Every day is a new adventure when travelling and the day I am going to recount is a typical example. I had wild camped overnight at Glomfjord, on the Northwest coast of Norway. I was heading to the Lofoten Islands by ferry the next day, but today I was going to explore a little where I was. I had arrived late in the afternoon and hadn't had a chance and I never leave a place without exploring.

I had seen a few cars driving up the mountainside the day before and wondered where they were going, so I decided to investigate. Not far up I found a carpark overlooking a river with a walk that ascended the side of the mountain. As soon as the walk began, I had to face one of my fears of crossing over a rickety wooden suspension bridge fairly high over the river. Fortunately, it was only short.

My rickety bridge over the river

After that it was a fairly steep climb up a narrow path traversing the side of the mountain. At some points I felt my stomach getting anxious because of the steepness of the drop by the side of the narrow path but I was determined to press on. I always know I will be rewarded with incredibly beautiful views, especially in Norway.

After my walk I returned to the van for lunch before heading off on my day's drive. I normally only drive for a maximum of three hours but prefer to only do two, especially when it is on winding roads as it generally always was in Norway. But today it was only going to take about an hour and a half to get to my next destination of Reipa. Before leaving Bergen, I had roughly worked out each day's journey so that I could have a week in the Lofoten Islands, before then heading to Tromso to meet up with Adam. So, I literally just look at the map and see what places are near to my route and stopping time and then use the Park4night app to locate a nice place. But as I get close to my destination, I am always scanning for nice spots, so if the Park4night location isn't to my satisfaction I have other options. And this is exactly what happened this day. I saw this beautiful location.

Reipa

I couldn't wait to get out and explore along the water's edge. There was this incredible island that I wanted to get some photos of. It reminded me of a Jurassic island where dinosaurs might live. I have a very vivid imagination. All along the water's edge were giant boulders to step across, and there were so many varieties of sea birds wading and flying around.

Whilst out exploring I went to take another photo of the island and couldn't find my phone. I suddenly remembered that I had put it down on a rock when I had taken a rest and I just must have forgotten to pick it up. Panic started to set in. I'm sure you must have experienced losing your phone at some point, but losing it on a beach where there are literally thousands of rocks was an impossible feeling. I'm normally pretty good in a crisis, and my mind will think rationally about the situation. All I could do was try and retrace my path across the rocks to find it and had already decided that I couldn't leave without it, even if it took hours to locate. As I walked back, I was thinking about what if I couldn't find it. I was all alone in the middle of no-where and it made me suddenly feel very vulnerable, having no way of contacting the outside world. I didn't even know if there would be any phone shops on the Lofoten islands where I could buy a new one. Friends and family would start to worry within a couple of days if they did not see any social media posts from me. And how was I going to contact Adam? I hadn't written his phone number down anywhere and I wasn't sure it would have been backed up yet as I hadn't had wi-fi for a long time.

However, after about ten minutes I saw it, sitting exactly where I had left it. I can't tell you how relieved I was. When I returned to the U.K. later in September, I found an old phone of mine so that if this ever happened again, I would at least have a backup. So that was my excitement for that day! I returned to the van for my regular afternoon cup of tea, although it was way past tea time, more like wine o'clock! However, I hardly drink alcohol when I know I will be driving the next day, something that I thought was a wise choice and also leads to a much healthier lifestyle. And my appreciation for a nice glass of wine or a gin and tonic is so much more when I do indulge.

In the times between exploring and driving, which can mentally be very tiring, I will take time out to just relax. This could be just sitting in a chair outside the van simply taking in the nature around me, reading, writing my daily journal or playing guitar (something I decided to learn whilst travelling). But there are also often jobs to be done, like writing blogs or editing videos for my YouTube channel. And chores like washing clothes or the van. Something I do when I have a source of water and of course washing myself. In Norway I would swim in the fjords to get clean, although even on the warmest of days the water there is pretty icy.

Dinner time would be when I started to feel hungry and once all the clearing up is done, I would sit and watch the sunset, my favourite time of day. I have witnessed so many amazing ones on my travels.

Like dinner, I have no particular time for bed, just when I'm tired and I've been known to go to bed as early as 8.30pm! or be up until 3am. It is a wonderful feeling never really having to worry about time or having to rise early.

Chapter 25
Beyond Rejection

For the most part though Adam made me feel like a princess, truly loved and adored. He did warn me though that he was flawed and not worthy. I didn't know at the time exactly what he meant by this, but of course I was to find out later in our relating that he would never be able to find the space for me in his life. But for now, it was perfect. He asked me what he could bring with him to Norway; supplies of food that I couldn't get or were expensive. Such a thoughtful request. And he brought my LPG converters with him that I had got sent to his home. He literally saved my life, as if I hadn't of been able to fill up the gas I would have possibly frozen to death in the van when the temperatures plummeted to below zero degrees later in September.

I was so full of nervous excitement to meet him. The night before was incredible; It was the night I got to see the Northern Lights for the first time at Laksvatn fjord. It was early in the season so they were not so bright but it was still amazing to be a witness to such a spectacular phenomenon. Another bucket list experience ticked off. I would be fortunate enough to see them another three times over the next month, although sadly not with Adam.

I ended up being a bit late to pick him up at Tromso airport, very unusual for me to ever be late. There was a diversion in place and I couldn't drive through the tunnel so I had to drive over the high bridge, which I was trying to avoid. Have I mentioned that this is one of my biggest fears? Heights in general but also high bridges, although by this point, I had, as you can imagine, driven over quite a number of them on my journey thus far. Norway has more tunnels than bridges but it still has its fair share of them. This particular bridge was to become my friend as I ended up driving over it six times in my journeys to and from Tromso.

Adam was waiting for me outside the terminal. My first impressions were great, he was gorgeous. We hugged and I kissed him gently on his lips. I knew he was an introvert so didn't want to overwhelm him with excited exuberance at finally meeting him. I felt so at ease with him from the moment we met and I was in a very calm and relaxed space. As we filled up the LPG there was a double rainbow over Tromso, the perfect way to start our journey. I was to see a lot more rainbows in the coming month in Northern Norway and on my way to the Vesteralen archipelago, the northernmost part of Nordland, I saw six in one day!

Adam was in awe of the snow-capped mountains. I could totally relate to how he was feeling because not one day went past that I wasn't in a wow moment with the spectacular scenery that is Norway. We caught the ferry to Senja, a small island off the northwest coast, north of the Lofoten Islands. And parked for the night in a layby right next to the beach, just ten minutes from the ferry terminal. It turned out to be the most perfect spot. We watched the sunset (yes, finally a man to share it with) and I cooked us salmon for dinner and a blissful evening of lovemaking ensued. Adam is a very considerate lover, dominant at times but always serving my every desire. I am learning to more gracious in receiving than I have ever been.

Van door view

The next day we just played van life, simply hanging out together. Adam was eager to help in any way he could so I tasked him with washing the van. Something I do at every opportunity to keep on top of the dirt. We collected firewood and made a fire in preparation for that evening and laid out on a blanket in the sun on the grassy bank next to the water, until we got a little too amorous with each other so retired to the van… and never made it back outside; it had started to rain.

The following day we drove to Tungeneset, where there is a beautiful wooden board walk on to the beach with a backdrop of the pointed peaks of the mountain range.

We couldn't stay long as they were blasting falling rocks on the mountainside! We headed for lunch to a fish restaurant at Mefjord where we delighted in eating fishcakes and whale for the first time! which tasted more like liver than fish. Glad I tried it but it's not something I will choose to eat again; liver is not my favourite taste. For dessert we had strawberry cake with a raspberry sauce and ice-cream. This was only the second time on my trip to date that I had eaten out and it tasted orgasmic. I had such an appreciation of being spoilt and Adam is in his element when he is eating good healthy food. Definitely the way to this man's heart.

Mefjord had the perfect spot to park, right at the edge of the fjord surrounded by mountains. At sunset the sun reflected on them turning them golden.

I was so happy. Every day was more beautiful than the last. Every day Adam told me how amazing I was and that he loved me. I was just being very present with it all. I was already sensing that our relating could be quite volatile to outside sources, no matter how he was feeling for me in that moment. I would need to just go with the flow of it. At least I would be fully satiated for a while by the time he left and that night he gave me the most orgasmic experience.

Our last day together was fabulous. Adam worked in the morning, and it was good for me to see his focus.

There was no room for me in this part of his world. But when he was done, we had the most amazing fish soup back at the restaurant.

Followed by a walk along the fjord to a cave, Adam relished in washing his face and hands with the pure fresh water from a stream. He was leaping around on the rocks like a child and I loved seeing him so free and happy. This is what nature and love do for you. On the way back I suggested we climb over the large boulders along the shoreline. He was a bit hesitant at first but I encouraged him to follow me. It wasn't long before he was having fun and way ahead of me. I was actually being a little more careful as I had become more aware whilst travelling that it would not be good to get an injury, so I just took things a little bit slower.

By the time we got back to the van it was 8pm so we got the bed out and ate strawberries with Green & Blacks chocolate. We only had two small bars between us but Adam was hyper. He was so funny. We chatted lots, listened to music and made love twice that evening. We were ravenous and debaucherous. Adam allowed me to give him a lingam massage. A tantric practice that is focused on the pleasure of the man with no particular outcome, where there is a conscious exchange of energy in giving and receiving pleasure. Eventually we fell asleep.

Next morning, we were up early to get the ferry crossing back to Tromso in time for having a final meal together there before Adam's flight home later that day. This would be the last time I would be looked after by a man for a long time and the food and wine tasted so good. We visited the wooden cathedral which happened to be right opposite the restaurant. Apparently, it is the most northernmost Protestant cathedral in the world. As we were sitting in the pews with the sunlight shining on us Adam asked me to marry him. I said yes. Of course, this was just a story as we were both still officially married, although two weeks later I was to sign my divorce papers. Our names are in the cathedral visitor book.

Before Adam left, he gave me his lovely soft sweatshirt, thick cream hoodie that I had said I liked, his thick socks and natural toothpaste and moisturiser. So amazingly kind of him and I have worn and used everything on a regular basis. Another example of life providing.

I was sad dropping him off at the airport, but so happy for our incredible time together. We messaged a lot on his journey home and it seemed to take him forever as he had two flights and wasn't back in London until the early hours of the morning.

In the days that followed we messaged frequently. Adam was feeling phenomenal, his words, after being back in touch with nature and spending time with me. I was catching a flight the following week back to the U.K. for Gina's eighteenth birthday and Adam and I would meet up in London.

Meeting Adam in London didn't go according to plan due to his work commitments. We had arranged to meet at North Greenwich at 5pm so we could have a picnic in the park, in the beautiful warm sunshine. We eventually met in Canary Wharf at 8.15pm. Not to dwell on feeling disappointed I spent the early evening walking to Greenwich Park. The vista from the park across to Canary Wharf is a magnificent sight of historic buildings against a backdrop of modern architecture.

After resting in the park for a while I strolled back along the Thames whilst the sun was setting. It's an interesting path, pretty isolated and not somewhere I felt entirely comfortable walking on my own.

Adam wasn't hungry as his work colleague had convinced him to eat a burger and I was starving. He sat and watched me eat pizza at the hotel we were staying the night at. Both of us were tired, but once we got to the room and had showers, we were reinvigorated for our lovemaking. I'm not entirely sure why we didn't shower together. A lazy lovemaking morning, followed by a trip to Borough Market for lunch where we delighted in sampling different cuisines. Borough Market is London's most renowned food and drink market. Then it was time for another goodbye, if only I had known then I wouldn't see him again for three months, and only then for a few hours before I boarded a flight to Bali where I was to spend two months.

Chapter 26

Heartbreak & Death - October 2019

I was in Northern Sweden and had just dug myself out of a foot of snow when I learnt that a seventeen-year-old boy, in my daughter's year at school, whom we had first met in Nursery when Gina was three years old, had hung himself at the weekend. That day was the hardest drive of my life, having to contend with roads full of ice and snow, snow still falling and all the emotion of what I had just learnt.

I couldn't seem to stop crying. This distressed me in a way that I cannot fathom. I was distressed because he was so young and had his whole life ahead of him, yet he was so disillusioned with his life that he felt the only option was to end it. He couldn't see that he had choices, or that there were friends and family around him and that he only had to ask for help.

I have known three other men in my life who have also committed suicide, two work colleagues and a friend. Young people today seem to put so many pressures on themselves, and don't seem to realise that above everything else their happiness is of paramount importance.

I have no idea why this young man took his life, but I do know what it feels like to think that there is no alternative. When I was in my early thirties and living on my own in a flat in Brighton, I wrote my death note to my Dad explaining why I had taken my life. It was only the realisation, as I wrote it, of the pain and suffering I would put my family and friends through that stopped me that night from taking the pills I had lined up. I just couldn't do it to them. I have never told them this so I am sure this will be a shock for them to read. I feel very emotional just thinking about it.

Following that night, I went to see the doctor who told me I was depressed and that I would have to wait six weeks for six therapy sessions. I knew I couldn't wait that long and was recommended a therapist by a friend and paid for private therapy for two years, dredging through my life trying to find answers as to why I was now so depressed. It is only right now in this moment that I understand that it was my thoughts, based around fears that had been conditioned into me from my childhood and past relationships, with the consequence of me not loving myself or feeling deserving of love. That I thought that my happiness lay in the hands of others, in the arms of a man. If you don't love yourself you focus on someone else to make you feel loved. Most of us do it without even realising. I remember thinking if only I had someone to love me everything would be OK and when I did finally meet someone everything was OK, more or less, for seventeen years. I was content at any rate and had two beautiful children.

I think that you are probably beginning to see that being loved by a man is something that I desire in my life. I don't use the word need anymore, as I know that my happiness does not depend on a man, but myself. However, I'm not going to be all self-righteous about this and say that I have got it all figured out because I know this is still work in progress and probably always will be. There is always room for us to grow in love and understanding of ourselves.

Every relationship, be it friendship or otherwise, gives us such an opportunity.

Chapter 27

My online romance scammer

I like to think of myself as a reasonably intelligent woman, and am pretty savvy when it comes to online safety. I've spent years worrying about my children's safety online and whether as parents we were doing enough to protect them. And my daughter was a victim of both a toxic online friendship and grooming at one point. So, you would think that I wouldn't fall victim to a scammer.

Wild reindeer - Skulsfjord

I posted a video of reindeers on Instagram and received a message from a man. I was fairly new to this platform and naively thought it was someone interested in my video. My age group are still mainly Facebook users. I checked his profile out, Michael Murray, and it said he was a zoologist. Not only was he gorgeous looking, he was a French/Australian with a very sexy French accent. He looked authentic enough, although had only been on Instagram, with this account at any rate, for three months. This didn't bother me at the time as I had only been using my account for a few months, since travelling, but I now know this is a big red flag. Instagram accounts setup by scammers are generally only there for a few months as they get reported. In that moment when I accepted his message, I made myself vulnerable. It wasn't long before he asked to move to Google hangouts which I had no idea about, but turns out its similar to WhatsApp but uses your email address, so you never actually have a phone number. This did not raise any red flag to me at the time and in some ways is less intrusive as you do not exchange your actual mobile number, but as I have now learnt this is a platform used by scammers.

Our first conversation was pretty long and he mentioned about looking forward to meeting my kids (which I ignored) and he did ask for some sexy photos (which I ignored). OMG! Why do men do this, and on the first chat. A high value man would never do this as he would be more respectful. In that moment Adam saved me by messaging me. When I told Michael this, he got seemingly jealous and started asking lots of questions about this friend. I lied to him, to make a hasty retreat from our chat. Told him it was a friend I would be staying with in the UK. I made my excuses to leave the conversation and his message was "Please don't forget to dream about us all night long, okay love" with loads of emojis. I wasn't looking for an online romantic relationship, particularly with someone who lived so far away. And I was relating with Adam, and was just about to spend time with him in London.

The next morning, I sent Michael a message telling him about Adam as I did not want to mislead him and I wasn't feeling comfortable with the way the first conversation had gone. A few hours later I got an online bunch of roses with the message "Good morning to the most beautiful woman in this world. You are the queen of my heart, and I cannot imagine my life without you." He told me he was happy and respectful of my honesty, but he did ask a few questions about Adam but wished the both of us the best luck ever. When I wished the same for him the conversation took a dramatic turn. "I don't want to meet any woman again; it's better I stay this way. I fell in love with you but not knowing that you already have someone". He fell in love with me after one conversation! As I write this, I see the craziness of that moment.

Even so I kept conversation going with him but on a very non-committal level as my priority was Adam despite his lack of engagement to my messages and Michael was being very attentive. I recognised even at this point that something wasn't quite right with how attentive he was being. I had never experienced a man who wanted to message so much, exactly what I desired, so I guess I wanted to ignore this red flag. And the red flag that he was online in the early hours of the morning – Melbourne time

My journey continued for the next month through the entire length of Sweden to Stockholm, Denmark to Copenhagen, Germany, Belgium, France to Versailles and Bordeaux, Spain to San Sebastian, Granada and Almeria.

Adam eventually gave me some hope that I would see him again at the beginning of November in Southern Spain. But his lack of communication and then informing me at the last minute he could come for the weekend, and me being too far from the airport meant that it just wasn't going to happen. This was to change my relating to Michael as I opened to him more despite me noticing yet another red flag. We had a phone conversation and he didn't sound the same as on his Instagram videos even though he had a French accent. I of course made reasons up for why this might be.

I arrived in the small town of El Toyo, Almeria in Southern Spain in early November and found the perfect place to park, right next to a palm studded beach with a beautiful view of the mountains on the other side.

Apart from a few other vans and a few locals it was deserted as it is a summer golf destination. This was where I was going to take time out of driving, for at least two weeks. It was pretty perfect, with showers on the beach and a water tap nearby. Time to be with myself and process the last few months of travel. But everything was not to go to this plan.

I met a couple of the other van dwellers, an English and a Frenchman. I loved the Frenchman's way. He had a huge van and was travelling with his two dogs and two cats. They were both headed to Roquetas de Mar and invited me along. I was a little hesitant but decided to go as they told me you could park directly on the beach. It was stunning.

Roquetas de Mar

I then did something crazy following a conversation with Michael. I booked a flight to Melbourne from Gatwick on Christmas day. He had told me that he wanted me to come and I had wanted to go to Australia for a lifetime. I was blinded by the whole story I was weaving for us and his two young daughters. And I thought, worst case scenario is that I would finally get to see Australia, even if it didn't work out between us. I was so excited, but when I told him, he said he was flying to Guyana that weekend for work and that I should cancel it! He had told me that this was in the offing but he would be home for Christmas. Fortunately, I had done the sensible thing and added cancellation insurance but I was able to easily cancel the flight as it was within the first twelve hours of booking. Red flag number four! But at least he had some conscience to tell me to cancel it as of course he would never have been at the airport to meet me.

I sometimes wonder if constantly living in a dream life removes you from reality. I certainly often feel on the outside of what I call 'the real world'. So then when reality hits it's a bit of a shock.

My relating with Michael progressively got more intense. I would be messaging with him into the early hours of the morning and each morning he would send me beautiful messages. I was opening my heart completely and was so trusting, although I did feel he was a little crazy. How could a man be so infatuated with me when we hadn't even met? Of course, it wasn't craziness, he knew exactly what he was doing and I was blinded by all the attention he was giving me.

It was at this time that I met with a Spanish girl, actually the girlfriend of the Englishman. She was a beautiful girl but was suffering severely from depression and had absolutely no self-worth. She wanted to spend time with me and although it had its nice moments of sharing between us it became very draining of my energy. I also started to feel very anxious and it triggered all my memories of when I was depressed. I was in a very vulnerable place which is why when Michael asked me for money, to release his equipment from customs for his job on the oil rig, I couldn't see the lie that was unfolding right before my very eyes. I'm shaking my head, as you must be. Apparently, scammers often pose as oil rig workers, doctors and military. I had never bothered to read about scammers as I thought I was aware enough to prevent it from ever happening to me.

A couple of days before this he had rung me in the early hours of the morning and we had phone sex, something I don't ever remember doing before. It was actually really nice hearing him turned on whilst we talked erotically together. He said I was the best wife ever?! He called me this because that was what he wanted me to be.

I can see now that this was part of the bigger plan, have phone sex, make me feel even more vulnerable and then tell me he didn't have enough money to get his equipment from customs. He had also asked for pussy photos that night but I refused to cross this boundary of mine. I have since learnt that scammers will use these photos to blackmail you at a later date. I was so naive to this so thank goodness I stuck to my boundary.

He never actually asked me for the money, I offered it. These guys are skilled conmen. I wasn't entirely stupid though as I only gave him as much as I could afford to not have returned but it was still £1700. There was of course a time pressure involved so I did not have time to think much about it. Such a good ploy – text book. But I was fully aware and putting my trust in that he was genuine but at the same time acknowledging that it was entirely possible he was not. Even knowing this I had formed a stronger attachment than even I knew. His attention was also keeping my mind off the fact that I was not hearing from Adam.

Michael had been messaging me continuously. Telling me how he had never really felt love until then. I was in this fantasy story with him except wanting it to be a reality. We talked about how our life would be in Australia living in our beach house. When you believe your dreams can be a reality there is nothing that can stop you. Now you may think this is a dream like desire but I have made my dreams a reality on a number of occasions so I know what I am capable of.

What is more, during this time, I told Adam I no longer wanted to be in our conversation alone. That his lack of communication was the death of us. I was glad I was no longer fearful of the outcome as it needed to be said. If someone wants to relate with me then they need to stay in communication, connecting.

I loved this tree on the beach at Roquetas de Mar

A couple of days later my world came crashing down when Michael asked me for some more money. Of course, I told him I had no more to give. It was the dawning of the realisation that he actually was a scammer. I hated the thought that the phone sex was him just getting off on one and all his words were bullshit. I've since seen videos of Guyanese men just mimicking orgasm which I have to say made my stomach turn knowing that there was a vulnerable woman at the end of the phone and maybe this is what happened with me. But I still didn't want to believe this was true with Michael.

This is when I started to investigate his Instagram activity and I messaged one of the women who was also following his ten-year old daughter. I found out that he was talking to multiple women and spinning the same conversation. One was a journalist and was doing a piece on romance scammers. He was one of them. She asked me not to report him just yet and I decided to continue communicating with him to try and gain more insight now I was in a position of power. I asked him for a video which he said he would do, but of course it never materialised.

When I received a message from his ten year old daughter's account, so obviously him messaging, I knew I could no longer continue with this charade. It was time for me to let go so I blocked the accounts and deleted hangouts. I was heartbroken as it was me finally accepting the truth. He was a scammer and not even the person on his Instagram account just some French Guyanese man. At the time I was holed up in the hills somewhere near Cordoba, with very intermittent phone signal and poor weather. It was the perfect place for me to release all the stress and upset that had been building up over the past couple of weeks. I had been so gullible and I completely understand not how this can happen.

My hide out in the hills near Cordoba

I started to inform myself by watching YouTube videos about these men and could understand why they felt like this was a good way to earn money. But they have no idea of the anguish they leave in their wake. And probably don't even think to care about it. It is just business to them, nothing personal.

My mind then took a strange turn. Remember what I said I do in times of emotional instability? What if I could find the real man? The man whose Instagram account had been hacked. There was a lot of photos of him in Bali and he was definitely a pilot. I read on google that a lot of pilots who work for the Asian airlines live in Bali and the photos and videos seem to confirm this. I even managed to locate where the rock islands were in Bali where several photos of him and his dog were taken with them in the background. This is when I thought, why don't I go to Bali. It was another place I had always wanted to visit. I knew someone who lived there who I had met on the India retreat and another friend was going to be there at the same time. To me it was suddenly the place I thought I should be.

So, me being me, reacting from an emotional state, I booked a flight to Bali leaving the U.K. on December 27th to stay for two months. I had worked out that the accommodation costs would be no greater than the spend on fuel for the van and I knew food costs were low. The thought of having this to look forward to helped me through this emotionally difficult time.

But I was also busy in my life with my journey through Spain to Cordoba, Seville, Almonte, to the Donana National Park, Punta Umbria and finally to Portugal.

Chapter 28

My Aura - Portugal December 2019

Swallows flying high at sunset

We arrived at the secluded almost deserted beach of Praia de Albandeira in time for the sunset. When I say we, Raimon had flown out to spend five days with me in Portugal before I headed back to the U.K.

It was the most perfect spot and we parked on the cliff top overlooking the beach. There is a magnificent rock archway formed from the erosion of the sea which we walked to the end of to sit and take in the sunset. It was a little uncomfortable sitting on the edge of the rocks so I decided to go back and get the rug and a beer from the van so we could watch the sunset in relative comfort. After I sat back down Raimon shared, that as he had watched me walking back towards him, he saw me surrounded by my aura of green and purple, moving along with me as I walked. Raimon said I was like an angel, just what Adam called me. It was a magical sharing moment and I was ecstatic at the thought that my vibration of energy was strong enough to be seen. He has never seen an aura before, neither have I and I have since read that it is very unusual unless you have been trained.

Colour is a wave travelling through space. Our eyes register different colours of the electromagnetic spectrum based on the space between the peaks of the waves. The brain interprets these spaces between waves into colours.

We see an aura because the energy bodies are vibrating at different frequencies and these are seen as colours in the auric field.

A green aura indicates growing compassion, love, and a desire to be of service, to help others. It is a colour of balance, harmony and a feeling of that I am OK, you are OK, everything else is OK. This colour reflects personal growth, openness of the heart, willingness to change and transform.

Purple indicates that a person is integrating the physical plane and the spiritual plane. It indicates a blending of heart and mind, as well as a sense of leadership. It indicates intuition, high imagination, visualization, and connection to the world of dreams. People with purple aura have an ability to lucid dream, astral travel and other psychic abilities.

Wow, seems that my aura is a true reflection of my current self.

Chapter 29

Christmas in the UK 2019

After Raimon left I had ten days to drive 2000km back to the U.K. to catch the Eurotunnel on Christmas Day morning. It seemed to rain for most of the entire journey so I was not feeling the joy of travel. It was a very surreal feeling on Christmas Eve night parked up on the wet and windy cliffs of Boulogne overlooking the bleak English Channel. There were a few other people there too and of course I wondered what brought them here on this night. Christmas Eve for me would normally be spent with my children and this would be the first time that Santa would not be bringing them a stocking overflowing with all those gifts that only he knew they would love.

I was feeling so emotional. A few more hours of driving were all that was left for a couple of months. I was sad to be leaving 'Lucy'; she was my home after all. And I was questioning why I wanted to go to Bali, so far away, when everyone I loved was in the U.K. I just felt I was meant to go there.

As I drove off the Eurotunnel the sun was shining on what was to be the most beautifully sunny day. England was welcoming me back with a smile for sure as I headed to Brighton where I was to spend Christmas Day with Raimon. Following my last year's Christmas with Joss, it was a somewhat different experience, but altogether fabulous. We drank champagne (something I always do Christmas morning), had a lovely walk along Brighton seafront and returned back to Raimons's flat for his homemade vegetable broth.

He had even bought a miniature Christmas tree for the table especially for me. So thoughtful. After lunch we recorded 'Merry Christmas Everyone' by Slade with Raimon playing guitar and posted it on Facebook. Just a sharing of love and happiness. We talked about his trip in March to Vienna and Budapest and he asked if I'd like to go with him. So, I booked a seat for £30 on the same flight to Vienna. Little did we know then how in just a few months the world was going to be a very different place to live in and we would never make that trip because of Covid 19.

When I left the next morning, we were both very emotional with tears in our eyes, at yet another goodbye. My next stop was to see Zach. Gina had decided to fly to Lithuania to spend Christmas with her boyfriend. It was so lovely to spend time with him and we had a lovely lunch of cold cuts left over from Christmas Day with Nick, his partner and my mother-in-law. It's so great to be able to have a harmonious relationship with them. Something very few couples achieve following separation. And I felt happy in the knowledge that my children would be well cared for.

Chapter 30

Escape to Bali

On Boxing Day morning, I get a text message from Adam saying 'I want to see you'. I had told him on an earlier conversation in December I was back in the U.K. for two days, never expecting to see him as it was Christmas. I messaged him back telling him the only possibility would be at terminal four Heathrow airport after 10.20pm. I heard from him at 9.17pm, saying he was coming and he would get us a room at the hotel there for the night so we could spend a few hours together in comfort. He told me he had missed me so much and true to his word he arrived at 11pm.

It was so easy with him. I am very good now at just being in the moment and flow of life. We chatted for quite a while, sitting on the bed, me crossed legged, and eventually we lay down next to each other. He stroked the skin on my back and gradually we became more amorous. I needed to ask him the question as to whether he had just met with me for sex. I'm not sure what drove the need for that question when I knew the answer would be no. I guess because I needed validation as he doesn't take the time in his life to stay connected with me. He said "No" and that we need not even have sex if that is what I wanted. But, in that moment, I wanted to have that intimacy with him. I needed to feel loved.

That night I saw a childlike quality in him, requiring constant reassurance. I believe he experienced a body orgasm as he was in ecstasy whilst I was giving him pleasure. He told me after that it was the most phenomenal experience ever. It was a very intimate night and the last time I saw Adam.

My journey to Bali was long as I had a layover in Amsterdam and by the time I arrived at the timeshare in Candidasa I had been travelling for thirty-six hours. I had decided to use some of my timeshare weeks as a treat to myself. I needed to utilise them as after thirty years of owning them, with the van I wouldn't really have the need for them and it is an extra yearly cost I could do without. Over the years they have served me and my family well and definitely have saved much money on holidays to some fabulous destinations.

Bali was so hot and humid and the traffic congestion with scooters and cars was crazy. It wasn't quite, at first appearance, the paradise island I had imagined it to be.

However, after being in the van for so many months my room felt like pure luxury. Big comfy bed, huge bathroom with a hot shower and a swimming pool surrounded by palm trees right outside my room. This felt like a holiday although my mindset was still in traveller mode. It was a reasonably expensive resort by Bali standards, but cheap for holiday makers. However, for me it was outside my budget so I had to be strict with how I spent my money. The local shop was not well stocked for someone who only had a microwave to cook with but they did bizarrely have fresh pasta dishes and pot noodles. So, this is what I mainly lived on with the odd meal treat at the hotel when my body yearned for something a little more substantial.

My room was just at the far end of the pool

The beach at the hotel was not great, black sand and the tide was in a lot of the time which meant you couldn't walk along it. However, the view of the rocks that were in Michael's photos was perfect and their formation reminded me of a whale. When I had first seen them in the background of photos of the resort, I was amazed at the coincidence and it was a little surreal to see them in reality. I wasn't able to work out exactly what beach along the coastline there Michael had been on, and without getting in a taxi to take me to each and every cove I wasn't going to know. And even if I did find it, was I really expecting to bump into him? I was in reality enough to know I should give up on this crazy idea.

Mountains at Candidasa with Mt. Agung behind

Three days after I arrived it was New Year's Eve and plans were afoot at the complex for an all you can eat barbecue, live music and a fireworks extravaganza. The Balinese people really know how to put on a great celebration and the attention to the detail of the decoration was to be admired. This would be the first time I was away from home and not with friends for New Year so I was expecting to be emotional at some point. I dressed up in the white dress I had treated myself to, after a fair amount of deliberation, in a sale in Antwerp and felt sexy and glamorous. I was one of the only single people there so was feeling a little awkward especially when I saw I had been given a table for one! I had made friends in the few days I had been there so I knew I would not be on my own for long. I need not have worried as I ended up sitting with a lovely Indian couple, about the same age as myself, that I had met earlier in the week and they were great company.

It was a fabulous night. Fireworks were shot from every resort complex along the coastline and from the island of Nusa Penida opposite. A night to remember for sure. Except for one thing, just after midnight I kissed this Australian guy, who was there with his wife but she was in bed ill. Sometimes I do stupid things when I've been drinking and I drank a lot that night. I didn't even fancy him. A pitiful excuse I know and I'm not proud of myself but his marriage was not my responsibility. Later in the pool he wanted to get close with me but I told him no and eventually he gave up and left the pool but after I had gone back to my room, he knocked on the door. I didn't answer to start with hoping he would simply leave but when he didn't, I opened the door and told him to go away. Hopefully he was glad of it the next day and fortunately, they left a couple of days later. I had managed to get through the New Year without shedding a tear.

The people of Bali are so friendly and kind, look at you with grace and ease and always with a smile. They take time and care in all they do. They don't rush, work hard and do even the most mundane tasks with pride and dedication. The majority of Balinese people are Hindu and it is so beautiful how they honour the Gods with offerings every day, in and outside of their homes on the streets, and even on scooters. The creation of these offerings models the generosity, faith, and devotion that exists in the hearts and souls of the Balinese people. These values translate into everything they do and everything they are. Something we could all model ourselves on.

Offering on the street

After two weeks of Candidasa I went via Lempuyang Temple, "The gates of Heaven", at sunrise to Nusa Dua. The temple was a little disappointing as you are not allowed inside, but the view across to the live volcano of Mt. Agung was stunning.

Lempuyang Temple

This is one of the most famous Instagram spots in Bali as you strike a pose in front of a pristine pool of water that reflects the sky above it. Except, this is all trickery done by a mirror placed under the lens of your phone.

Nusa Dua beach area has been commercialised into a touristic sanctuary for luxurious holiday accommodation with exclusive beach resorts, landscaped gardens and long stretches of glorious white sand beaches backed by palm trees. I of course was staying in a cheap hotel just outside of this more expensive exclusive area. The only reason I was staying here was to get my visa extended. If I had known it was going to take three weeks I wouldn't have bothered to stay here as it was too commercialised for my liking.

However, it did give me the opportunity to have my very first surf lesson at Nusa Dua beach. I was so nervous about it as I'm not a great fan of being out of my depth in the sea. I have forever been affected by the film 'Jaws'. But it looked like so much fun that I wanted to give it a try. I was impressed at my ability to ride the very first wave that my instructor put me on and I think he was pretty impressed too. I have a great sense of balance, having ice skated as a teenager and then inline skating when I lived in Brighton. I even appeared in a skating magazine, which is actually how I met Nick. He saw my photo. The hardest thing for me was paddling back out into the surf. It was pretty strenuous and after an hour and a half I said I had done enough. I spent the rest of the afternoon crashed out on my bed.

My next week was spent in Uluwatu at the accommodation of a Brazilian lady, Bhuvana, whom I had become friends with at the tantra retreat in India. I love how when you travel it opens so many doors to being able to visit and stay with people you meet along the way from different countries and cultures. I had the best time socialising with everyone staying at the accommodation.

Uluwatu is a beautiful, very untouristic part of Bali with some gorgeous white sand beaches, good surf and the famous Uluwatu temple with its monkeys.

It was in Uluwatu that I got my second tattoo. There was a tattoo shop right next door to where I was staying and before I had arrived in Bali, I had already identified my next tattoo so it just felt like the perfect time. It is a Chinese symbol meaning 'Who we really are' as I had a real sense now of who I really was as a person and showing up as my most authentic self.

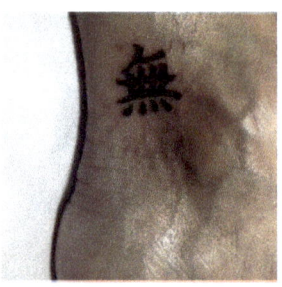

Then it was onward to Ubud, in the centre of Bali. The terraced rice paddies are among Bali's most famous landscapes.

This is an epicentre of mindfulness for visitors and expats alike to congregate. There are many retreats, ceremonies, workshops and yoga classes to join. I participated in a Kudalini yoga class, my first. A magical science that uses sound, mantra, energy healing, exercise and meditations to release trauma from the energetic body, which surrounds the physical body. Kundalini yoga helps us recognise that abundance is our birth right and living from our hearts is the surest path to prosperity. It brings balance to the body, mind and soul. Although I love the idea of it in reality it is a pretty strenuous workout when you are not used to it.

My first week I stayed at the same place as my friend from France, Amelie. She is also a friend of Ray's and we had been chatting online so when I was travelling through France in October 2019, we met up in Bordeaux so that she could experience van life for a day. Something she had always wanted to do. It was great spending time with someone in Ubud who knew the area and such fun travelling around on the back of her scooter.

One evening we participated in a Cacao ceremony. This is a type of shamanic healing where you drink cacao. I'm not sure what I was expecting to happen apart from being energised. But in fact, it had the opposite effect of a warm and fuzzy feeling. However, the whole ceremony was beautiful. We sat in a mother womb tent in a sacred circle, taking prayer, singing and sharing gratitude. I was very outside of my comfort zone but I embraced and enjoyed the experience.

Ubud very much reflects the heart of 'Eat, Pray, Love', a film with Julia Roberts partially filmed there amongst the rice paddy fields. I had not seen it but coincidentally it suddenly appeared on Popcorn, which I had on my laptop, so was able to watch it whilst I was there. It reminded me of my journey, except I didn't go to Italy first to eat! But I did go to India. And I didn't find the man of my dreams in Bali either, although I had plenty of offers. But if I was to share myself with anyone it would need to be with someone to whom I felt a real connection and it just didn't feel so genuine with the Balinese men. There was one Brazilian man I met who I was drawn to and I did let him know that I was attracted to him. Even though nothing ensued I felt liberated in that I was able to tell him my truth, albeit by text message. When your heart is open and you can communicate your inner feelings without any expectation of any particular outcome you know you are being your most authentic self, being with your truth.

The real highlight for me of Bali was my trip to the north of the island to the mountains and jungle in the Munduk region.

View from my room

My room literally overlooked the huge expanse of the jungle and mountains behind. I half expected to find monkeys on my balcony.

This is where the spiritual twin lakes reside, Tamblingan and Buyan, surrounded by many temples. There were few tourists there in the month of February and you could freely walk through the rice paddy fields and jungle where there are many beautiful cascading waterfalls. But even though these waterfalls are remote there is still a person there to collect your money. And it was in fact at one of these waterfalls that an old Balinese woman completely ripped me off with the price. Later when I realised, I went back to get my money and I could not believe that she denied overcharging me. It made me feel really upset as I had been so trusting and she took advantage. Maybe a little naive on my part, lesson learnt.

It was here that I ventured out on an amazing overnight canoeing and jungle camping tour with one other lady from India. We experienced a real piece of uncommercialized local life. I sat around a fire that night with six Balinese men, who were there to look after our every need, drinking the local brew. I was on fire, just opening my heart. I have no idea what they thought but they seemed happy enough to listen and I learnt so much about Balinese life and culture. It was a real privilege to be part of such a unique experience.

Wanagiri Pucak Manik Waterfall

After two months of experiencing Bali, it was time to head back to the U.K. and resume van life. I originally had a direct flight home but this got cancelled and I had to reschedule my flight twice and ended up having to take three flights. This was just as Coronavirus was starting to take hold in Europe and my flight from Jakarta to Amsterdam was eerily empty with a row of seats for every person. Very few people were wearing masks at this point and I was not feeling fearful in any way.

Chapter 31

Why do I need to feel loved?

It's April 2020 and I'm writing this from the house that I used to live in with my family before I separated from my husband. Lucy is parked up on the driveway.

I am inspired to write today because of the freshness of this feeling I am having 'Why do I need to feel loved'?

Why am I even here in a house I left two years ago? Well because of the Coronavirus, Covid 19. On my return from Bali at the end of February Coronavirus had already taken its hold in China and was beginning to start to spread across the rest of the world. Two weeks later the U.K. was put into lockdown.

To distract myself from my feelings for Raimon, I decided to revisit the dating apps. I'm not really sure why I was suddenly desiring him more again. Maybe because of the wonderful time we had spent in Portugal together. I matched on Bumble with a thirty-five-year-old Portuguese man, Ricardo. It seemed quite apt as I was intending to head back to Portugal in the van as soon as the rules allowed. He looked gorgeous, don't they all?! He lived locally in Worthing, had a dog and loves to travel. What could be more perfect? I'm laughing as every man I match with seems perfect and that is far from the actual reality. However, they are perfect in that moment and each experience reveals more about myself. At this time, I was initially just looking for a distraction and some loving connection as with lock down we were not supposed to travel or meet up with anyone.

We had been chatting for a few weeks on a regular basis and had arranged to meet on a weekend but then he had to sort out getting a new fridge, so he postponed. Then he lost his job due to Coronavirus and then it turned out that he needed to leave his current place and move back to his old flat so I was going to see him today/tomorrow.

But he didn't message me yesterday and he's not been on Instagram since then, which seems strange so I'm now thinking is he with someone else? Then I ask myself the question 'Is this really true'? I don't know that it is, so why am I trying to cause myself pain with this feeling of rejection. Like I'm not good enough, when I know I am. I had so much expectation, although I was trying so hard not to have in case something happened. It's like I'm always expecting something to sabotage my relating. I feel physically sick inside, tears are welling up in my eyes. The 'Why does this always happen to me feeling'? Well, I know why. It's because seemingly I am still not attracting an available man. This just reflects that I need to do some more inner work. The coronavirus government restrictions have taken away the ability to meet anyone (although I was going to meet with Ricardo) and I don't like video calling if I haven't already met. I'm scared that I won't come across as my most authentic self. So now I have all the time to concentrate on myself.

It seems there is always more inner work to be done on loving yourself more and understanding conditioning from past trauma. I am trying to be more forgiving of myself and not keep validating the thought I'm stupid for being so open. This is the only way to find true love, making yourself vulnerable and not being afraid of having your heart broken.

And I know I haven't even met this guy but I already felt attachment to him and we had talked about our sexual preferences quite openly. He had invested a lot of time relating with me which is why what happened next took me completely by surprise.

I never got to meet Ricardo. That same day he blocked me from his Instagram account and removed me from Bumble. What an arsehole. That was the day I learnt what ghosting was. Maybe I was never chatting with the real Ricardo, but if I wasn't, he was good, had a whole story. He did me a favour really as I was only repeating old patterns with him and he was evidently not 'my man'.

Chapter 32

My Corona Virus Birthday May 10th

Well, we all know that life can be completely unpredictable and never more so than right now. The U.K. and a lot of the world are still in lock down following the outbreak of Covid 19. Luckily, I had been able to catch up with a few friends before it was imposed.

It's not a good time for vans to be parked up in beauty spots so Nick suggested that I park my van on the drive at the family home. He was at his partner's house in Kent with my son Zach and had decided to stay there so that I could stay at the house with my daughter and my mother-in-law. Now I can hear your gasps at this! But I lived in this house for twelve years with my parents-in-law. Mother-in-law is in a self-contained separate part of the house and keeps herself to herself much of the time. We take it in turns to make dinner and all come together then, so it works well. And it is so peaceful here without the boys in the house although I'm missing not spending time with Zach.

My plan had always been to come back to the U.K. for April, when my house rental was coming to an end, so that I could redecorate before getting new tenants. Also, to sort out my finances so that I could continue to travel without an income. I have now given an extension on the rental of my house until the end of July as I wouldn't have been able to get new tenants at this time with the social distancing measures in place. I managed to have a couple of sessions of osteotherapy on my neck and back but that is now on hold and Lucy has not been able to have her service.

I am embracing this time to continue with writing this book, exercise and often just do nothing, just being with this period of stillness and healing for the world. I am grateful that I can walk straight from the house into the surrounding countryside and we are all fortunate in the southeast of England that at least we had been blessed all Spring with glorious sunshine. Although I do feel that I have been pulled back a little into life's conditioning and having responsibilities that I do not want. Like cooking for others and cleaning a house. I also had it in my mind that I would like to date someone whilst I was back here. I am missing sexual intimacy. However, there seems no point to pursuing that here right now as I want to head back to Portugal for the winter months. So instead, I have been connecting with men in Portugal who I could have a relationship with, not just a 'fling'! So there seems to be some nice potential there and I have discussed with a few about meeting up. Of course, there is no lack of emotionally available men anywhere. We just need to be in the right energetic flow to attract them.

My actual birthday consisted of sharing cake, Black Forest Gateaux, at Gina's request, and a glass of wine in the afternoon with her and Sylvia. I then headed to Brighton to spend the rest of the day with Raimon. We drank champagne, ate cake and played monopoly – five games. He just couldn't get ahead of me. He cooked a very tasty salmon and pasta dish and the following morning gave me a healing hands massage. Not a bad way to spend a lock down birthday, and yes, I was breaking the rules by seeing him.

Chapter 33

Lock down Virtual Dating - May 2020

Filipe was one of the first Portuguese men that I matched with on Tinder at the beginning of April. Our relating started really nicely. He immediately asked for my mobile number so that we could connect on WhatsApp. He's wasn't too young either, forty, tall and of course, gorgeous looking. He has a good job and is contemplating buying a house now he's back in Portugal. He's spent a lot of the last ten years working out of the country. Our first couple of chats were great. I found out quite a lot about him and though there were a couple of sexual innuendos there were no seedy comments, as can be the case with a lot of men. He's into photography so we had a discussion about that as I was keen to learn how to use the Sony camera I had bought. He refers to when we meet a lot and that's always a good sign. Although I've had a couple of occasions when men have said this in the past and it's all been a story. But if I let this make me closed to trusting other men I meet online our relating will never go anywhere.

Then he did the thing that a lot of men do, and sent a dick picture with the comment "Every centimetre of my body will be very happy to be yours. Just wanted to let you know". It did make me smile as he is cheeky and he actually has a very nice cock. From then on, our conversations had more sexuality in them, but in a flirtatious and open way towards sexuality. So often we are afraid, ashamed (without even realising it), to talk about our sexuality. It is one of the most natural ways of human connection and sharing of love. Unfortunately, he had not been well since we had started chatting and his messaging started to tail off. I just gave him the space and he messaged me about once a week to give me an update.

Then three weeks later he's back full on asking me if I would like to watch him take a shower on a video call! Guess he was feeling better. I was completely taken by surprise by this offer, not something that had been suggested before by anyone. But, when he asked if I was free in that moment, I said I wasn't. Mainly because I was not prepared bodily as of course I knew that he would like me to share something in return. Actually, I preferred this option over men asking to see pussy pictures or videos. At least I would get to meet him in a very open way. I think lockdown probably opened the way for people to be more explorative in the virtual world.

I'd assumed that we would rearrange our virtual 'date' for the next day but he had a valid reason for not doing so but didn't communicate this. I had much nervous anticipation all day until late afternoon when he told me he had already taken a shower in the morning. He said let's try tomorrow so yet again I had to endure another day of anxious excitement in the pit of my stomach, waiting to hear from him, as I want him to be in the same desirous state as I was in. No point chasing if he's not in the right energy even though he was the one that suggested it. I never heard from him. This was a turning point in our relating and I told him I no longer wanted to share this experience with him. If he couldn't be thoughtful enough to let me know there was a reason why he wasn't showing up then he is definitely not the man I should be sharing myself with, especially virtually, no matter how attracted I am to him. And I do wonder if I was fully happy to share in this way or whether I was just trying to please him. I was very sexually charged; I think because there was a full moon rising in my star sign. I'm always highly energised when this occurs.

I have also been messaging with a number of other Portuguese men, that I met on Tinder and match.com. Every experience is different, and I am now looking on it as a way to learn more about myself and to work on those triggers in dating that I find difficult. Like attaching too quickly and getting anxious when I do not get a reply to a message. Learning just to lean back in my feminine and wait for the man to move the relating experience forward.

This can be challenging for me as I am an anxious dater as my fears of abandonment and rejection get triggered so I often try to drive forward the relating, by messaging if I haven't heard anything or in dating needing to know when our next date will be. Not very in the flow I know. So now I see myself doing this I can exercise a certain amount of control. I have boundaries though so if waiting for that next text message feels like it is compromising my boundary, I will send a message. But not in a chastising way, but in an invitational way to reconnect. But there are only so many times I will do this, as if they are not voluntarily showing up, I know I have to let go of the relating as it will only bring me pain to continue. And this letting go of course can be challenging also.

I had started to message every day with Miquel. He's fifty-nine, reasonably good looking, has hair – which is always a bonus with an older man. He has been and is on a very similar path to me. Divorced two and a half years ago, has two children, aged fourteen and sixteen. His hobbies include hiking and cycling as well as sailing. Two of the things I most enjoy and the other something I would certainly be willing to participate in, despite my fear of deep water. However, he does apparently need his space to do his own thing, which may be why he doesn't currently have a woman in his life. He retired as his job was no longer fulfilling his existence, I love he made that choice. He seems to be financially secure, so has the means to spoil me with the odd meal out although I'm pretty low maintenance. He is also looking to buy a third property in the Algarve and has offered to help me look for some land. He's trying to be my 'hero' already and does appear to be an emotionally available man. In his own words, he is honest, trustworthy, open and transparent, positive, always in a good mood, happy and playful (think he stole that from my assessment of myself), kind, caring, romantic, loving, tactile, sensual and sexy. Almost exactly the same as me, though apparently not stubborn or bossy like I can be. He enjoys campervan travel, rented a van last year with his children, and also has been travelling on his own since he had his new found freedom. He was meant to be going to India this year but had to cancel because of Covid 19.

We do appear to be very well matched and currently he is showing up for me every day. Now all we need is that chemistry attraction, which I hadn't yet felt. He has been very respectful in his messages, with only the odd wink here and there. He is very much in the present and not creating too much of a story for us. This is something I realise I do, create a story of a future before I've even met the person. I am checking in on myself with this every time I feel myself doing it. I actually enjoy imagining how a future would look together but I just need to not make it so personal to the guy. Just imagine it to be 'my man' with no particular form.

Relating nicely in this way is exactly how it should be, not men sending pictures of their cocks! Although, don't get me wrong, I quite enjoy a nice cock picture and I am always interested in the size and shape. But if you see it in the moment when you are actually already in a lustful state, if it's not quite up to expectations, then it doesn't seem to matter nearly so much. After all it's how the man shows up in intimacy that is of more importance, not the look and size of his penis. Although a nice looking one is always more appealing of course.

Yesterday 24 May 2020 I found out that Spain and Portugal are planning on reopening their land borders on June 16. Brittany ferries are running a service three times a week from Portsmouth to Santander and Bilbao. I have decided to book the ferry for Monday June 30th, Zach's fifteenth birthday, but it is a virtual school day so we will celebrate the day before. I'm holding off booking, for a couple of weeks to ensure that the border closure does not get extended as it looks like Spain's state of emergency is being continued until the end of June. This is perfect synchronicity.

Chapter 34

The Life I want to Live

I have been listening to some mindful podcasts recently about living the life you want to have. For me this would include living my life as if I have 'my man' already in it. The rest of my life is exactly how I want it already, no real plan, but to travel more in the van and possibly buy some land or a house in Portugal to have as a home base. And give myself the opportunity to be in one place long enough to meet 'my man'.

The first question I ask myself is 'What relationship am I looking for?' and the second question is 'How is having that in my life going to make me feel?'

I want a conscious relationship. A relationship when two people come together with the intention of growth. A partnership where we have an opportunity to expand more together than we could alone, where deep satisfaction and long-term fulfilment arise as a result. Well, that's the mindful part.

I want to be adored and be one of my man's highest priorities. I want a man who wants to take care of me, be my protector and hero. A man who can communicate their needs and desires and to listen to and value mine. A man I can grow in love with without being attached to an outcome. I want to be able to be my most authentic self and have space to express those feelings and fantasies. This is one of the most healing things we can experience in a partnership, when we know we will never be judged.

It's rare for anyone to be completely honest about who they are and what they feel. And if it is communicated, we may not like what we hear and it may trigger all sorts of past trauma emotions. But this is the only way to have a true and authentic relationship.

I don't want to be afraid to be myself for fear of losing my man's love for me.

In my marriage I wanted my husband to act in a certain way, I repressed myself to please others and I lost my true self along the way. The relationship felt like a cage that I wanted to break free of 'Fly free'. I now know it was me that caged myself. It was my entire responsibility and I lay no blame. It was my conditioning of wanting children, a husband, a house that led me down this path.

How do I feel having this man in my life when I know he physically isn't present? Currently only in my dreams. I know I would feel so happy, smiling all the time, having that warm glow in my heart knowing that anything is possible with this man by my side. Funny thing is, I know all of this should be true now whether he is in my life or not. This is what I have been trying to achieve. This was the whole point of my journey. To be happy with myself, living the life that I choose. And I am happy but I choose now to have 'my man' share this amazing journey of life with me.

And why is it so important for me to have a man in my life? To feel cherished and loved, to feel known, seen and truly understood. To have an outlet for the love I have to share. To share hugs, make love and have playful fun.

I am seeking a lot I know, which gives me the fear that I may never find it. But I truly believe there is an abundance of available men out there. I just need to find one of them.

Love is a journey, not a destination, just like life and I will continue along this amazing path of life loving myself, doing what makes me feel happy, sharing love and kindness with everyone I meet and hoping to inspire others to live their lives to their fullest potential.

If you are not attached to an outcome, whether that be in a relationship, sex, work etc. you give yourself the opportunity to grow to your full potential and experience the fulfilment of being in the present moment. After all, how do we know that we will be here tomorrow.

Chapter 35
And Now?

I had been listening to Madeline Charles, a relationship coach, about becoming the 'Irresistible Woman' and attracting the right man. Everything she said resonated with me and I realised that if I truly wanted to find 'my man' I was going to need some help.

I have come such a long way in 'loving myself' and knowing who I really am. However, although I can identify why I have trouble in attracting emotionally available men I still go down the same old path. Being attracted to the men that are 'emotionally unavailable'. That craving for emotionally charged excitement. But with that always comes heartache, because they are just not able to fulfil my emotional and physical needs.

Despite having no income and knowing that this was almost my entire month's travel allowance for food and petrol, I signed up to her yearlong 'Irresistible Woman' coaching course. Wow, I really believe that

I am worth investing in and committed to really finding 'my man'. I know most people would think this was a waste of money, but it is no different to buying any product that helps you look and feel great. I look at how much money friends spend on hair colouring, makeup and clothes. I have never really been a person to honour myself in this way, maybe because I didn't feel deserving of it. I always felt guilt when buying something new, if I didn't really need it. It felt frivolous and actually still does, more than ever now.

But I'm not feeling frivolous about this. I'm feeling excited about what is to come. Following an hour zoom call with her she believes that finding someone will happen quite quickly for me as I am so available and open to it. Little did I know then how much about myself I was about to discover.

Two weeks later I matched with Jony on Tinder. When I first saw his profile a week prior, I swiped left as I felt too attracted to his bad boy image. Motorbike, piercings and tattoos, but he had the most gorgeous eyes and beautiful face. He looked strong and was tall, unlike a lot of the other Portuguese men I had been chatting with and I've always been more attracted to a taller man. He was what I would call a man's man. I thought that he would not be that high value man I desired. We know that we should never judge people by what they look like, but still, it's hard not to form an image in your mind.

We had a really interesting first chat and no mention of anything sexual or sending photos. Even Jony remarked on it. I guess women are keen to get a man's attention by sending sexy images. I've done it myself but only normally if I'm asked. At the end of our chat, he gave me his phone number. After that he messaged me every day, a lot, some days we chatted for hours. Then we started to have calls as he liked to hear my voice. We talked about so much, about our lives, about dreams and love and today we had a virtual walk together. He was walking in the beautiful hills around where he lives on the Setubal peninsular and was sending me videos and photos whilst talking on the phone.

This is what I want. A man who really desires to be sharing with me. I have never had this on such an intense level before, apart from my romance scammer. I am loving every second of it although it's been quite exhausting. I should tell Jony this as I know him well enough already that he wouldn't want me to feel like this, but yes, I am fearful of him feeling rejected. But it really isn't my place to be responsible for that, only myself, but…

The reflection of all my needs and desires is right there in Jony. He is in the present moment with me for sure. Today he told me he loved me. I laughed, out of shock, I think. I quickly apologised as I recognised the tone in his voice was so sincere. He explained that if he feels something in the moment, he says it. It is the same for me. I was feeling love for him, in context of course, as we hadn't even met, but was not going to tell him for fear of scaring him. One thing for him to tell me and another for me to reciprocate. This reminded me that I was not being my most authentic self and that I absolutely should have told him. I have since on a video.

I'm in for one hell of a ride with him. Maybe he is 'my man'. But whatever happens I know that I will be giving myself the opportunity to love and know myself more than I do now.

Let's see.

Chapter 36

Escape to Portugal

On the 30th June 2020, the border into Spain reopened and I sailed on the first Brittany ferry to leave the UK, from Portsmouth to Santander. After having spent three months, mostly stuck in one place it was exciting to be finally back out on the open road. I was a little fearful too. Travelling to a foreign country on my own in the midst of a pandemic. If this wasn't facing fear's I don't know what was. Living in a van has its advantages in a pandemic situation as you have the freedom to travel and stay safe in your own home.

I needn't have worried, of course. The sailing was extremely well managed, with plenty of hand gel provided all over the ship. Masks were compulsory when in public areas and everyone had to have a cabin. Most people seemed to stay in their cabins and just come out to stretch their legs every now and again, as I did. Once we arrived in Spain it was a quick temperature check and a form to complete and I was away, free.

Jony had provided me with a recommended route as he had explored all the areas I would be driving through on his motorbike.

I headed to the Picos de Europa mountains in Northern Spain, the opposite direction to mostly everyone else, and after an hour and a half of driving I was back in nature and parked on the side of a mountain overlooking Cangas de Onis, the gateway to the Picos de Europa National Park.

I woke to this sunrise over Cangas de Onis

For the next fourteen days as I travelled down through Northern and Central Portugal I was completely immersed in the gloriousness of nature with its stunning mountains, winding roads, lakes, sunrises and sunsets. What better way to begin the next chapter of my life?

Epilogue

The Princess in her Ivory Tower

As I stand staring from the third-floor window of the apartment in Palmela, Portugal (that I have rented for six months in order to get residency) at the mountains of Arrábida on this rainy day, suddenly, with tears rolling down my cheeks, I have an answer. It's so simple and I cannot fathom why I've not realised it before now. Or maybe it was simply I did not want to admit it to myself.

When I left on this journey, I did not believe I was running away but running towards a better way of living. But now I understand I was also running away. I was running away from the loneliness I felt inside myself. I was surrounded by family and friends that loved me, yet, I was still lonely. I think I have been lonely for most of my entire life. This forced time living in an apartment and staying still has revealed 'my truth'. And although I'm crying, I am relieved and grateful that I finally understand.

Travelling in the van has been so inspiring for me, just flowing along in the natural current of life. Being in deep connection with nature and myself. It has allowed me to reconnect with the person I truly am.

I also wanted this to be a love story. I wanted the knight in shining armour to come and rescue me. But I know he never will. Only I can rescue me with true love and acceptance of myself. Now everything is so clear. I have turned to men for intimacy to feel loved that takes away this innate feeling of loneliness that is within my very soul. I realise now that it has been the abandonment of who I truly am, and not showing up as that person that has caused this feeling of loneliness.

Now I am being who I really am and all I need to do is keep sharing the love I have in my heart and soul of life and myself and that will be fulfilment enough. That is being who I truly am.

The End